John Hill Hewitt

War:

A poem, with copious notes, founded on the Revolution of 1861-62

John Hill Hewitt

War:
A poem, with copious notes, founded on the Revolution of 1861-62

ISBN/EAN: 9783337732592

Printed in Europe, USA, Canada, Australia, Japan

Cover: Foto ©ninafisch / pixelio.de

More available books at **www.hansebooks.com**

WAR:

A POEM, WITH COPIOUS NOTES,

FOUNDED ON THE REVOLUTION OF 1861--62,

(UP TO THE BATTLES BEFORE RICHMOND, INCLUSIVE,)

BY

JOHN H. HEWITT.

————In a moment, look to see
The blind and bloody soldier with foul hand
Defile the locks of your shrill-shrieking daughter; ·
Your fathers taken by their silver beards,
And their most reverend heads clash'd to the wall;
Your naked infants spitted upon pikes;
Whiles the mad mothers with their howls confused
Do break the clouds.—*Shakspeare—Henry V.*

Mark where his carnage and his conquest cease;.
He makes a solitude, and calls it—peace !
n······n's Bride of Abydos.

RICHMOND, VA.:
PUBLISHED BY WEST & JOHNSTON,
NO. 145 MAIN STREET.
1862.

DEDICATION.

To James Barron Hope, Esq.

Dear Friend: Please excuse the liberty I take in dedicating to you the following hastily written poem, which I dare not dignify with the title of epic. The remembrance of past hours, of pleasant associations, the many kindly favors which I acknowledge at your hands; and more particularly my admiration for your shining merits as a scholar, a patriot and a gentleman, have induced me to inscribe these pages to you.

You will find, on perusal, much to condemn as bordering on the doggerel—but you must be aware that when a poet is bound down to *facts*, he is compelled to throw the *ideal* aside; at least, I have found it so in attempting to chronicle the events of the war in rhyme.

Yours ever,

THE AUTHOR.

INTRODUCTION.

The election of a sectional President, and one, too, an acknowledged enemy to the institutions of the South, in 1861, fired that portion of the happiest and most glorious nation in the world with indignation. The conservative element of both sections looked on aghast—they had been defeated in their endeavors to ward off the appending storm, and a majority of the electoral vote proclaimed Abraham Lincoln, the Abolitionist candidate, President elect of the United States of America.

South Carolina was the first State to deny the authority of a purely sectional chief executive ; she raised the banner of "rebellion," and was followed by the rest of the cotton States, Georgia, Alabama, Louisiana, Mississippi, Texas and Florida ; the border States, Delaware, Maryland, Virginia, North Carolina, Tennessee, Kentucky, Missouri and Arkansas, remaining *in statu quo*.

During the interim between the election and inauguration of Lincoln, the seven cotton States prepared to resist the threatened coercion of the United States. They armed themselves and seized the forts, arsenals, armories, ships, war materials, &c., of the Federal Government, and secured themselves against invasion. Troops were mustered into service and instructed in camp duty, and the youth of the city and the rural district rushed to the standard of the Southern Confederacy.

Major R. Anderson, the commandant of the forts in Charleston harbor, was summoned to surrender the property under his charge. He at the time occupied Fort Moultrie. Assuming acquiescence to the demand, he put the "rebels" off their guard, and suddenly changed his quarters to Fort Sumter, a new and strong work in the centre of the harbor. This act of duplicity greatly exasperated the people, and a determined siege was commenced. Thousands of troops were called ' to Charleston ; strong batteries were constructed on every available point around the stronghold of the Federalists, and all intercourse with the main land or sea cut off. This fort remained in a beleaguered state until the 13th of April.

In the meanwhile the Southerners had taken possession of many of the military works on the coast of Florida. Fort Pickens resisted, and was besieged in a like manner as Fort Sumter. It was reinforced by the Federal Government on the 11th of April, and also protected by a large naval force.

On the 4th of March Abraham Lincoln was inaugurated President of the United States. His address on that occasion, defining his position, was considered, even by the moderate men, as equivalent to a declaration of war against the South. He denied the right of States to govern themselves; urged that the United States was *the* Government, and that independent sovereignty was a mere myth. These doctrines were, of course, scouted by the South, and the war fever became more intense.

The border States, in the meanwhile, endeavored to allay the rising storm. Virginia had called a State Convention; plans were proposed by the leading men of the border States; some of the conservative men even of the seceded States threw themselves into the breach, and suggested conciliatory plans. Commissioners were sent from Richmond to Washington to propose plans of settlement—a Peace Congress assembled at the latter place, and wise and grey-headed men implored the Executive and his advisers to act with moderation and listen to the just and honorable claims of an oppressed people. It was all in vain; fanaticism ruled the councils of the dominant party, and the institutions of the South *must* be crushed out, it mattered not what the cost might be.

The Confederate Government sent to Washington Commissioners to negotiate with the United States Government, and to settle, if possible, the points at issue. These Commissioners were detained day after day, and ultimately received their dismissal without accomplishing anything. By this delay the Cabinet gained time—their plans, though hurried, were carried out, and war, with all its accompanying horrors, was determined upon. The Commissioners were induced to believe that Forts Sumter and Pickens would be surrendered to their rightful owners without resort to powder and ball, but the policy acted upon by the Federal Cabinet was based upon deceit and villainy, if men are to believe the exposures which were subsequently given to the world. One of these exposures was the inhuman determination of the Federal Cabinet to sacrifice Anderson and his men, in order that the North might be fully aroused to the necessity of pushing the unnatural war to a bloody extreme.

The Commissioners returned; and on the 12th of April the South Carolina batteries under command of Gen. Beauregard opened on Fort Sumter, and a bloody and protracted war was inaugurated.

CANTO I.

A sullen murmur, like the moan of waves
That circle round old Ocean's hidden caves,
Comes on the feverish air; now louder still
The sound swells out o'er valley and o'er hill,
Until it falls, like thunder on the ear—
Stirs the proud soul and strikes the churl with fear.
On, in his barb'd and fiery-steeded car,
With Death and Rapine, rushes angry War,
Flaunting his blood-red banner in the wind,
And laughing at the crush'd hearts left behind.
The vulture soars above his reeking track,
And lightning shafts are flashing at his back;
While from his car-wheels issue thunder tones
That blend with shrieks and dying warrior's groans.
He calls on man to slay his fellow man,
And points to glory as his rich reward;
Laurels that flourish in the bloody van,
Reap'd by the strong arm and the weeping sword.
Then up, ye sleepers!—'t is the loud decree,
Repel the foe—or live in ignomy:
Famine and fire—the bayonet—the ball
Must be withstood; obey your country's call.
Ye may not see old age—but then, ye may
From Fame's high temple tear the crown away,

And live in story or in graceful song,
Your grave the Mecca of th' admiring throng.
Aye—this is glory for the chief, but none
Trace honors on the soldier's grey headstone.
Arm, then, for right—for home—for those you love,
The good's in doing what your hearts approve;
Leave fame to those whose ears invite the sound,
Your duty is to yield no space of ground:
For, what is war but strife for mastery?
    The gates of mercy close—while passions riot;
Hosts clash with hosts, like billows of the sea,
    And where there's desolation there is quiet.
War is the god of some men; wreaths and crowns
Are pluck'd from cannons' mouths and burning towns;
Their deity, tho' clothed in robes of blood,
And scattering terror over land and flood,
Looks smiling in their eyes, and, like the sun
Warms into life the flower it shines upon.
Perchance it's so—but *brothers*, when they meet,
Should have a hand and not a sword to greet;
And let our anger guide us as it will,
A brother has a brother's feelings still.

'Mid orange groves, in mountain passes wild,
O'er pregnant fields where bounteous Nature smiled,
In busy marts, the battle cry rings loud
From godlike lips amid the surging crowd.
The Southron answers to the stirring call,
The vale—the plain—the hill—the dazzling hall,
Send forth their bands of youthful chivalry,
Strong in the right, determined to be free.

Old rifles, sabres—rusted o'er by time,
Borne when our patriot sires were in their prime,
Once more come forth and shine in bright array,
Ready to do—when brave men lead the way.
　There sat all mute a Southern maid—her eyes
Were fill'd with tears—the heart's sweet memories
Were spoken in her sighs—joys past and gone—
A weeping flower,—a lute without a tone.
Beside her stood a youth—his lofty brow
　Bent downward, while his flashing eyes betray'd
The burning love he scarcely dared avow,
　But well he knew the call must be obey'd.
He grasp'd his father's musket in his hand,
　His mother's Bible rested on his heart—
"I go," he said, "to shield my native land,
　But ere I go I'd say how dear thou art.
See on the plain my young companions throng,
Their banner in the breeze—their swelling song
Invites to conflict.　Would'st thou have me stay
And not be up at Freedom's dawning day?
Virginia calls—the hireling hosts have press'd
Their iron heels upon a mother's breast;
Her golden fields are trodden—desolate,
Her people feel a tyrant's deadly hate!
Maid of the South!—dearer to me than life,
Would'st thou consent to be a craven's wife?"
The maid arose—shook back her raven hair,
Her eyes shone bright, but not a tear was there;
Firmly she grasp'd his hand, and whispered "No—
This is my off'ring to my country—go!"

2

What pen can tell a mother's love—what song
Can speak the fondness, durable and strong,
A mother wraps around her child—her joy,
The hope of coming years, her darling boy?
She gives him to the cause, the widow's gift,
And bids him high his country's standard lift,
Strike for his home—his rights; and, should he fall
An angel host will bear his funeral pall.
    The young wife fills the homespun haversack,
Buckles the knapsack on her husband's back,
Kisses his sun-bronz'd cheek and weeps awhile,
Then, scorning tears, she summons up the smile;
Gives him her babe and bids him kiss once more
The little treasure ere he goes to war.
Proudly she scans him and his rifle too,
For well she knows they both are staunch and true,
And bids him go and join the doubtful fight,
The strife of Southern right and Northern might.
    They mount their restless steeds, the Ranger band,
With carbine slung and shining knife in hand;
Over the prairie, thro' the shadowy glen,
Up hilly slopes, on speed those fearless men.
The rocks send back their wild and piercing cry,
While the proud eagle leaves his roost on high,
And, half afright, joins in the elfin song,
Mocking the war-cry as he soars along.
Gathering, still gathering—from river swamp,
    From jungle wild, from glen and lofty crag,
Until they mass in one far-stretching camp,
    And crowd around the Southern rainbow flag.

Brothers are there, and hoary-headed sires,

   And beardless youths, and pretty vivandieres;

One pulse, one glow the common soul inspires,

   In Freedom's cause the high and low are peers.

The young and beautiful with patience ply

The needle for the soldier's canopy;

While gray-hair'd matrons knit with trembling hand,

To clothe the heroes of their Southern land;

Aye—lisping babes are taught the wild refrain

That brings the faint heart back to life again.*

Hark! from old Moultrie's cannon'd embrasures †

Belch streams of flame, the angry war-dog roars,

---

* The homely air of "Dixie," of extremely doubtful origin, though pretty generally believed to have sprung from a *noble* stock of Southern stevedore melodies, became spontaneously the *national* tune. The words are uncouth and unmeaning; some patriotic verses have however been wedded to the mongrel melody, and have proved stirring. The children in all sections of the Confederacy were taught to sing it, while at the North to do so was treason.

† On the night of the 12th of April the Confederate batteries, under Gen. Beauregard, opened on Fort Sumter, in Charleston harbor. The fire was returned by Major Anderson, then in command, and the bombardment continued throughout that night and the next day and night, 36 hours. The flagstaff was shot away by our guns; and soon it was announced that "Fort Sumter was on fire." A flag of truce was displayed, and Col. Wigfall, who was appointed Aid to Gen. Beauregard, went with a white flag to offer assistance to extinguish the flames. He approached the burning fortress from Morris' Island, and while the fire was raging on all sides, effected a landing. He demanded that the Union flag must be hauled down or the firing would not cease. This was done, and Sumter surrendered to South Carolina—the firing then ceased. Anderson and his men sustained themselves bravely, and they were allowed to honor the old flag with a salute as it came to the ground; this salute caused the death of four soldiers by the bursting of a gun—the only blood that was spilt during the affair. The venerable Edmund Ruffin, of Virginia, discharged the first gun from the iron battery at Cumming's Point. He subsequently shot all the guns and mortars used during the action.

And murderous shells sweep, humming, thro' the air,
Bursting in fragments—scattering everywhere.
On Sumter, lo!—the starry banner flies,
    The proud Palmetto streams o'er Moultrie's walls;
Both give defiance to their enemies,
    And tell of triumph—when the other falls.
Peal upon peal, the red shot flying fast,
    Like burning meteors rushing thro' the sky;
The dun smoke rolls—the heavens are overcast,
    And sea waves roar in uncouth harmony.
Sumter awakes, and, thundering, answers back,
The iron hail speeds on its airy track;
Louder the roar—old ocean's billows groan,
While sea-birds shriek in wild and mournful tone.
All day, all night the stubborn fight goes on,
Another sun lights up another morn,
And still the cannon chant their thundering song,
The howling shot speed fearfully along.
The Union flag has fallen in its pride!
The sign for which so many braves have died.
Sumter's on fire!—the flames dart up the sky,
Volumes of smoke rise in dark majesty—
Her guns are hush'd, the white flag now they raise,
Our batteries no more send forth their blaze.
Hail, Beauregard! whose peerless genius plann'd
The first great vict'ry of the Southern land.
Sumter has fall'n, and Carolina's sons
Have fell'd her flag and hush'd her monster guns.

    Swift thro' the land the thrilling tidings sped,
The blow was struck—the first blood had been shed;

The Union totter'd—loud the call to arms,
The drum was beat—the trumpet's wild alarms
Summon'd the hirelings of the lordly North .
To seize their arms and push their standard forth.
Thro' every loyal State—thro' every town
Where lived the memory of the traitor Brown,*
The call was made for fearless men and stout, ,
To coerce States and "crush rebellion out."

The orator arose with pliant tongue,
He touched the *feelings* of the motley throng;
Spoke of the Union, Constitution, laws,
Of Southern "rebels" and their hellish cause,
The God-forsaken, starving mob—whose hope
Was fratricide, whose end would be—a rope!
The "stars and stripes," the noble sign of old,
Must be sustain'd in every stitch and fold;
From Maine to Texas, waving proud—sublime,
From that day forth until the end of Time.
And then, oh! strange consistency! he told
Of dark-eyed maidens, hoards of yellow gold,
Rich farms and slaves, by Nature's birthright free,
All should be theirs who proved their loyalty.
"Booty and Beauty," was the Vandal cry,
The burning brand, the knife of crimson dye;
A servile uprise in a peaceful home,
Where discontent was never known to come.

---

* Alluding to John Brown, who was convicted and hung prior to the war, for treason against the State of Virginia. His daring raid upon the unprepared citizens of a member of the United States, and his vile endeavor to create a servile insurrection, won him the title of martyr from his sympathizing abolition friends.

The pulpit, where God's love should be the theme,
Was made the forge of mad fanatic's scheme;
Instead of prayers for sins to be forgiven,
Or supplicating peace—majestic Heaven
Was call'd upon to launch its holy ire,
To slay the rebel with consuming fire;
The cities, towns and hamlets, wherein dwelt
The traitor lips that utter'd what they felt,
The traitor hearts that beat for human right,
The traitor arm that dared to show its might.
Misguided thousands put their armor on,
 With martial drum and banner in the wind,
Gather'd around the powers at Washington,
 With vision'd spoils before and shame behind.
The vet'ran Scott, the man of many wars,
Who bore his honors thickly as his scars,
Shaped this vast host and made them fighters bold,
Fit to slay rebels—or to steal their gold!

Proud Baltimore! thou city of the fair!
Whose monuments arise in beauty rare,
Thine was the task to check the onward flood *
Of vaunting troops, thirsting for Southern blood.

---

* The first blood of the revolution was shed in Baltimore on the 19th April. The 7th Regiment of Massachusetts, attempting to pass through the city on its way to Washington to answer the requisition of President Lincoln, was assaulted with stones and other missiles by a mob. The soldiers resorted to the use of their fire-arms, and a general fight took place, in which several were killed and wounded on both sides. Gov. Hicks issued a decree calling on all good citizens to preserve the peace, and promising that no more volunteer troops from the North should be allowed to pass over the soil of Maryland at their peril. How he kept his promise, time shewed—it was violated in every sense,

"Back!" was thy cry, "back to your Northern homes,
Lo! from the South the cry of warning comes;
We'll greet ye with the bayonet and ball,
A grave upon the spot where you may fall."
From dwelling-house, from shop, from social board,
The people rush'd to meet th' invading horde;
And many a heart will mourn that fearful day,
And many a tongue recount the bloody fray.

Now turn we to a scene terrifically grand,
A work inglorious, wrought by flaming brand.
'T was midnight, and the quiet stars look'd down
Upon the wavy deep—the field—the town;
Nature was hush'd—the city seem'd to sleep,
While silence brooded o'er the sparkling deep.
Hark! there's a sudden boom—the night air quakes,
The sleeper, wondering on his couch, awakes.

---

and so exasperated the citizens that in their rage they destroyed four
bridges on the Philadelphia and Baltimore Railroad in order to prevent
the passage of Northern troops Fort McHenry was besieged by the
Marylanders. Gen. Scott appointed Gen. Patterson commander of the
District of Columbia military, while Baltimore voted $500,000 for the
defence of the city. At length the citizens seized upon all the arms
within their reach, firmly determined to keep the Federal troops at bay.
The military was completely organized and drilled, being under the
command of Gen. Trimble. At this point the treachery of Governor
Hicks became apparent. He issued a proclamation recommending that
the State occupy a neutral position; and this, too, in the face of the
fact that Federal forces occupied Annapolis, the capital of the State,
and were strongly posted at the Junction of the Washington and
Annapolis Railroads. He knew the serpent was slowly, but surely,
twining itself around his native State, so that no power, but determined
patriotism, could release her from its poisonous coils. In vain the
stout-hearted sons of chivalry grasped their weapons of death—their
enemies were allowed to crawl in among them stealthily, until Maryland was doomed to worse than slavery.

A streak of flame from Gosport flashes high,*
And darts its serpent-tongue along the sky:
The yard's on fire! the Pennsylvania burns,
Her heated guns spit forth their flame by turns;
While crackling ribs of mighty ships consume,
Five gallant frigates seek a watery tomb.
Roaring like angry dragons, spread the flames,
Devouring buildings, docks and vessel-frames,
'Till Desolation laughs—then all is o'er,
While Sorrow sighs and mutters—this is war!
But what cares man when passion has its sway?
Millions of wealth are madly thrown away;

---

* On the 19th of April the powder magazine at Norfolk was seized by order of Gen. Talliaferro. It contained 3,200 barrels of gunpowder, a large quantity of loaded shells, and immense numbers of shrapnel, shot and percussion caps. On the 20th a wanton destruction of Government property was perpetrated by the hirelings of Lincoln. The Navy Yard at Gosport had been watched by Virginia troops; this *guard of honor* did not exactly suit Com. Macauley's ideas of propriety, so he immortalized his name by an act of vandalism scarcely equaled in the records of history. Quietly the frigates Germantown and Merrimac were scuttled—the heavy shears on the wharf at which the former was laying were cut away and allowed to fall mid-ships across her decks, carrying away the main topmasts and yards. All the side and small arms were thrown overboard with other property. About midnight, after two or three slight explosions, the light of a serious conflagration was observed at the Yard. This continued to increase, and before daylight the demon-work of destruction was extended to the immense ship-houses, formerly containing the entire frame of the New York 74, and also the low ranges of two story offices and stores on each side of the main gate of the yard. The Southwest wind blew the flames directly towards the line of vessels moored on the edge of the channel, and nearly all these, too, were speedily enveloped in flames. The huge line-of-battle ship Pennsylvania also became a prey to the devouring element, and while burning, her heavy guns belched out and threw their shot upon the yard, thus completing the destruction. The Cumberland and Pawnee (the latter kept under steam) escaped. The vessels destroyed were the Pennsylvania, Merrimac, Raritan, Columbia, Dolphin, Germantown and Plymouth.

The toil of years is nought, when policy
Demands the act—no matter what it be.
Philanthropy—the word's not known in war,
  It shrinks with Mercy into silent groves;
While headlong Devastation mounts his car,
  Drives o'er the land and crushes what man loves.

In time to come, when Peace again shall smile,
  The lisping child may ask whose sturdy arm
First fell'd a foeman on Virginia's soil
  ·And died a martyr in the opening storm?
'Twas Jackson—he who shot young Ellsworth down,
And then was slain, all covered with renown;
A valiant man was he—a patriot bold,
No suppliant knee he bent, no pow'r of gold
Could buy him o'er, no threats could make him quail,
When he resolved he did not dream of fail!
  When Alexandria's streets rang with the yells
Of armed foes—as if a thousand hells
Had oped their gates and let their devils run,
The Southern flag stream'd brightly in the sun
Above his house.· He'd sworn that he should pay
The forfeit of his life who tore 't away.
The daring Ellsworth, with his Zouave band,
Climb'd to the roof and with unflinching hand,
Tore down the "rebel" ensign, trampled on
The glorious bars, and claim'd the trophy won.
  Flush'd with his vict'ry—burden'd with his prize,
He stood before the madden'd patriot's eyes;
Quicker than thought a bullet made its path,
And Ellsworth fell beneath the hero's wrath.

3

A moment—and a score of bullets flew,
Felling the patriot, bayonets pierced him through.
His gallant soul departed with a sigh,
Scorn on his lips, defiance in his eye.
  Thus fell brave Jackson; many as brave a man
Has since that day fall'n in the battle's van;
Many a youth, whose thirsting spirit drank
At Glory's fount in conflict's foremost rank.
Thousands still live whose dying shout will be
"Our homes all ruins—or our country free!"

At classic Yorktown—now a barren plain,
  A canvass city rose, and breastworks bold;
And oft the bugle's soft and silvery strain
  Woke the young echo in its rocky hold.
The stream stole past and dallied with the moon,
  While music crept along its stilly breast;
The soldier shelter'd from the heat of noon,
  Lounged on the grass and courted gentle rest.
The camp fire blazed, the ample kettle swung
On two cross poles, all dark and sooty hung,
While jovially the cook sang out his lay,
The song of Dixie Land, so far away.
The inner picket paced his trodden post
With arms at ease and in deep rev'ry lost;
His visor down upon his sun-burnt brow,
His bay'net glitt'ring in the sun's bright glow.
  Far off the outer guard his vigil kept
With ear awake each sound to intercept;
With eye that watch'd the motion of each limb
Of undergrowth in the far distance dim.

'Neath an old elm, whose giant arms spread o'er
  A pleasant lawn of long and wavy grass,
Loung'd officers, attached to various corps,
  Some puffing smoke, some passing round the glass.
The tale—the toast—the song of *Vive l'amour,*
The repartee—the laugh—the jocund roar,
Told of glad hearts, tho' danger lurk'd hard by,
Hearts that would bound at battle's stirring cry.
"A song! a song! to while the hour away,
And nerve our sinews for another fray."

SONG OF THE MOUNTED RANGERS.

The ball's in the tube and the carbine is slung,
The voice of our bugle has merrily rung;
And, champing the bit, each steed paws the ground,
As he hears the last note of that shrill bugle sound.
    To saddle! to saddle! then—up, boys, away!
    Ere the last star fades out in the dawn of the day.

Now, hear ye that crack? lo, the pickets are near,
The crags give the echo to bugle and cheer;
But little we heed, while yet we've a shot,
And a knife to strike home when the struggle is hot.
    Spur onward! spur onward! then—charge, boys,
        away!
    We are in for a brush at the dawn of the day.

We tramp o'er the plain, we speed thro' the glen,
Our steeds are the fleetest and stalwart our men;

The wheat-stack we fire and shoot by the flame
The Hessians who tarnish humanity's name.
    Upon them! upon them! then—charge, boys, away!
    Some blood will be spilt ere the high noon of day.

Bethink ye—our daughters, our sisters, our wives,
In the grasp of the foeman beneath their red knives;
Bethink ye—and on, while the life blood is warm,
And stern vengeance nerves the true Southerner's arm.
    No quarters! no quarters! then—on, boys, away!
    There will be a death howl ere the closing of day.

Up rose a son of groaning Maryland,
His canteen fill'd with native " contraband; "
Curling his moustache—throwing back his hair,
He sung his wild refrain with martial air.

SONG OF THE MARYLAND LINE.

We 're the boys so gay and happy,
   Wheresoe'er we chance to be,
If at home or on camp duty,
   It is the same—we 're always free!
    So let the guns roar as they will,
    We 'll be gay and happy still;
    Gay and happy—gay and happy,
    We 'll be gay and happy still.

We 've left our homes and those we cherish
   In our good old Maryland,
Rather than wear chains, we 'll perish,
   Side by side and hand in hand.
    So let the guns, etc.

Old Virginia needs assistance,
  Northern hosts invade her soil;
We'll present a firm resistance,
  Courting danger, fire and toil.
    So let the guns, etc.

Then let the drums and muskets rattle,
  Fearless as our sires of yore,
We'll not leave the field of battle
  'Till we've redeem'd old Baltimore.
    So let the guns, etc.

Happy that band, while lolling on the ground,
The jocund tale and merry laugh went round;
Stories of home, of fair ones left behind,
Of mothers tender, fathers stern, yet kind;
When the drum beat, and soon in bright array,
The martial'd host their polish'd arms display.
To Bethel Church—th' advanced post of the works,*
Within its range the bold invader lurks.
  Onward they march'd, and, when they reach'd the
      ground,
They threw up earthworks, fell'd the trees around,

---

* The battle of Bethel (or Big Bethel Church, as some have it,) was the initiatory field fight of the war. It was fought on the 10th day of June, at the place named, on the line between Elizabeth City and York Counties, Va. The Confederate forces, numbering between 1,800 and 2,000 men, were under the command of Col. J. B. Magruder (since promoted to Brigadier General), an accomplished soldier, late of the United States Army. The place is six miles from Newport News, sixteen from Yorktown, and eight from Hampton.

After several skirmishes, by way of prelude, commenced the pitched battle. The details of the Southern and Northern journals were very

Planted their guns, fill'd pits with riflemen
Commanding road and field and miry fen;
While Howitzers their brazen war-dogs placed
To watch the path the Yankee foot disgraced.

Magruder stood and watch'd th' advancing foe
Whose flashing bay'nets fill'd the pass below;
With clashing steel and polish'd tube they come,
With waving flag and beat of hollow drum.
"Down, down," he cried, "lay low, my gallant boys,
And when their front around that clump deploys,
Then give it them." Each hammer then went click!
The men so still—they scarcely seem'd to think;
Silence was eloquent—the bird of prey
Look'd mutely on, and soar'd far, far away.

The gallant Stuart on the breastwork stood　　•
And mark'd the Zouaves struggling thro' the wood;
They leap'd the fence—crawl'd onward thro' the brush,
Like stealthy cats, then made a frantic rush;
"Fire!" he scream'd; the Life Guard blaz'd away,
And many a widow mourn'd that bloody day.

conflicting—though the latter acknowledged a severe defeat and heavy
slaughter of their troops. At "Little Bethel" the Federals whipped
themselves in this manner: A German regiment, mistaking the signal,
fired on Colonel Townsend's column, marching in close order, who
returned the fire. Townsend's fire was harmless, but the Germans'
killed one and wounded two. Duryea's Zouaves hearing the firing,
fired upon the Albanians (Townsend's). In all five were killed and
quite a number wounded.

The battle was fierce; the enemy's force exceeded 4,000, and, strange
to say, our loss was only one man, with two wounded, while that of the
Federals amounted to hundreds. In this fight Cols. Magruder and Hill
signalized themselves, as also did the brave North Carolina volunteers
and the Richmond Howitzers. The fight was carried on altogether
by Virginians and North Carolinians. A Louisiana regiment arrived
from Yorktown too late to participate.

The howitz spoke at Randolph's loud command,
Mowing down ranks and tearing up the land;
While bursting shells threw devastation round,
And scatter'd mangled limbs along the ground.
   Men of the brave old North State! Where are they?
Look to the left where wildly swells the fray;
The cool and fearless Hill is there; his sword
Given to Death—his silent prayer to God.
Volley on volley—rifles true—carbines—
And quick revolver rake the staggering line:
They break—they fly—the cavalry pursue,
And slaughter, as they go, the vanquish'd crew.

Vict'ry now play'd around the Southern flag,
   With dazzling wings she fann'd its stars and bars;
Her cheering cry was heard on mountain crag,
   And echo'd in the vales with loud huzzas.
The beardless stripling panted for a fight,
While tottering age with locks of snowy white,
Sigh'd for youth's vigor—feebly rais'd his crutch
In mimic fight with Yankee, Irish, Dutch.
   In Kansas, Kelley met th' encroaching foe,*
And, with his State troops, laid their stoutest low;
While at Vienna, Gregg the foemen check'd,
Scatter'd their men—their cars and baggage wreck'd. †

---

* On the 17th June the battle of Kansas City took place. 1,300 Federal troops made an attack upon about the same number of State troops under the command of Capt. Kelley. After a desperate fight the Federals were repulsed, leaving 200 killed on the field of battle, 150 prisoners, four pieces of cannon, &c. Loss of the State troops 45 killed and wounded.

† On the 17th of June a severe affair took place at Vienna, about fifteen miles from Alexandria, between Col. McCook's 1st Ohio regi-

At New Creek, too, Vaughan, with Virginia's sons *
Caused them to fly before our Southern guns.
Near Romney, Ashby with a meagre band †
Of fourteen men fought bravely hand to hand
With fifty Hessians—thrash'd the thieving squad,
Leaving eighteen to bite the valley sod.

---

ment and other troops under Gen. Schenck, and a detachment of Confederate Artillery, supported by a South Carolina regiment under Col. Gregg.

According to accounts, Col. G. received orders to go on a reconnoitering expedition. He took with him 600 South Carolinians, a company of Kemper's Artillery and two companies of cavalry, including 45 of Capt. Ball's Chester company, and Capt. Terry's company, of Bedford. After ascertaining the position and number of the enemy, who were encamped on the Maryland side, he formed his command into column at Dranesville, and marched down the road to Vienna. Here he remained only long enough to tear up the track of the Alexandria, Loudon and Hampshire Railroad and destroy the water-tank, after which he started to return to Dranesville. The troops had proceeded about half a mile, when the whistle of a locomotive was heard in the distance; whereupon he immediately halted, wheeled his column and marched rapidly back to Vienna. They had scarcely time to place two cannon in position, when the train of cars came slowly around a curve, pushed by a locomotive. They were crowded with armed men. Just as the train was about to stop, the artillery fired a well directed shot from one of the guns, which raked the cars fore and aft. Consternation and dismay seized the Federals, and, after another fire, they hastily left the cars and took to the woods. The entire train was captured. Six of the invaders were killed—they were composed of regulars and Michigan volunteers. The National Intelligencer reported the killed and wounded of the Federals in this affair at 200.

* On the morning of the 19th June, an engagement took place at New Creek Depot, eighteen miles west of Cumberland, on the Baltimore and Ohio Railroad, between a body of Tennesseeans and Virginians, under Col. Vaughan, and about 250 of the enemy, who fired a few random shots, and then broke and fled. Our troops captured two guns and a stand of colors.

† This affair is thus detailed. As Capt. Ashby with his brother were proceeding along a road with 14 men of their troop, they were accosted by a man who represented himself as a deserter, and professed a willingness to conduct the squad to a position where they could take some

Then brave Zarvona, with his comrades plann'd *
A wild exploit which startled all the land. ,
He seized the proud St. Nicholas, and bore
His laden prize toward Virginia's shore ;

prisoners. The offer was accepted, the men proceeding on under the guidance of the deserter, till they arrived at a point in the road where the squad was divided, each half taking different courses.

Very shortly thereafter the deserter led them into a place where they were surrounded by fifty of the enemy, who called on them to surrender. This demand was replied to by a discharge of fire-arms, which was answered by the Hessians. In a short time the remainder of the squad rejoined their comrades, and united their exertions in repelling the enemy. In this they were successful, eighteen of the Hessians having been killed. Two of Ashby's men were killed, and a number wounded: Capt. Ashby received four wounds, and his horse fell dead as he was leaving the field which the enemy ran from, and escaped across a small river to evade pursuit. The brother, Capt. Dick Ashby, was fatally wounded. Turner Ashby was afterwards promoted to a Colonelcy, and fell nobly in the cause of the Southern Confederacy.

* On the 30th June, a brilliant and romantic achievement took place on the waters of the Potomac, which resulted in the capture of the steamer St. Nicholas, a brig and two schooners, the brig was laden with a valuable cargo of coffee, and the schooners one with ice and the other with coal. Col. R. Thomas (known also as Col. Zarvona), of Maryland, was the hero of this affair. Disguised as an old French lady, who could not speak a word of English, he took passage on the St. Nicholas, at Baltimore, for Washington. After getting down into the bay he threw off his disguise, and, with the coöperation of his men, who shipped as New York Zouaves, took the steamer. He was joined by Capt. Hollins, of the Confederate Navy, at Point Lookout, who participated in the capture of the other vessels. The other officers associated with Zarvona in the achievement were Lieut. Geo. W. Alexander, Adjutant, and Lieut. F. Gibson. These three headed the boarding parties in the captures. The steamer, after being placed in the hands of Capt. Hollins, who was assisted by Lieuts. Sims and Minor, of the C. S. N., and Lieut. Thorburn, of the Virginia Navy, with fifteen sailors from the steamer Yorktown, captured the brig and schooners, and proceeded to Fredericksburg. The value of the cargoes was estimated at $375,000.

Subsequently, however, he (Zarvona) had the temerity to visit Baltimore, much against the advice of his friends. As was feared, spies were watching his movements, and he was captured and imprisoned, not being allowed the privilege of exchange.

Three other barks, fill'd well with merchandize,
He brought in safe—a truly welcome prize.
Near Martinsburg again the foe was met,*
By gallant Jackson, who his front beset
With leaden hail, and many a wretch that day
Cold on the soil of old Virginia lay.

Our little navy, albeit, laurels won,†
Disputed every wave they floated on,
And spoke in tones of thunder to the foe,
"These seas are ours—no further shalt thou go!"

Now let fair Freedom don her sable weeds
    And mourn the gallant Dreux, who nobly fell ‡
With clustering honors, won by daring deeds,
    Shielding the noble cause he lov'd so well.

---

* On July 4th the Yankees, numbering about 10,000, while approach-
ing Martinsburg, were met by Col. Jackson's advance, consisting of a
portion of Col. Harper's regiment from Augusta County, about 700
strong, and a squadron of cavalry under Col. Stewart. A sharp fire
was kept up by the main bodies for an hour and a half, with a loss to
the enemy estimated at the minimum at 67 killed, 85 wounded and 53
prisoners—three killed on our side and five wounded. When the firing
ceased, Col. Jackson fell back to a more secure position.

† The Federal steamer Massachusetts, belonging to the blockading
squadron off the coast of Louisiana, had captured in Mississippi Sound
four small schooners belonging to the Southerners, and bore them off
as prizes. A body of Floridians, under command of Maj. Widsmith,
armed the small steamer Madison with two light guns, and, while the
Massachusetts and her prizes were becalmed off the coast, bore down
upon one of them, the Fanny, captured her and the commanding
Lieutenant, Selden, with the prize crew. The other schooners were also
taken possession of and carried into Suwanee.

‡ Col. Dreux, of Louisiana, fell in a skirmish on the Peninsula 6th
July. He was killed by a fire from an ambuscade.

At Phillippi a gallant Georgian band,*
Led on by Ramsey, took a fearless stand;
Foiled thrice their numbers, captured all their camp,
And made the boasters take the backward tramp.
With banners streaming, seven thousand strong
Came rushing on in columns dense and long;

---

* On the 10th July an engagement took place between the advanced guards or scouts, of Gens. Garnett's and McClellan's armies, near Phillippi, Barbour Co., Va. The first Georgia regiment, Col. Ramsey, encountered three regiments of the enemy, in which conflict the Federals were routed. The Georgians took a number of prisoners and all the camp equipage of the enemy. The Confederate loss was but two, while that of the Federals was about sixty.

This apparently small affair brought on the battles of Rich Mountain and Laurel Hill. The main army of the enemy advanced from Phillippi, and took up a position on the hill about half a mile from the Confederate post, which was, however, obstructed from view of the latter by a still higher hill directly between the opposing forces.

On hearing of their advance, our General checked them by taking possession of the hill on the left of them, and about daybreak the two forces commenced operations. The fight continued all day and part of the night with little or no result except the loss of many lives. During the night our forces retired from the field with the hope of inducing the enemy to follow so as to get them within range of our guns.

The brave stand made by our troops kept the invaders at bay for some time, but there was a reverse of fate in the conflict which took place the next day, the 11th, at Rich Mountain. A detachment under command of Lieut. Col. Pegram, which numbered only three companies, was employed in raising earthworks on the mountain slope. This small force succeeded in keeping in check, for some time, several thousand Federal troops, and although sorely pressed, not more than 40 were killed. The gallant Pegram was severely wounded and taken prisoner. Many of the men in his command, who were believed to be either killed or taken prisoners, afterwards reached Gen. Garnett's camp. Col. Pegram's entire command consisted of about 1,000, which were in three divisions, two of which were commanded by Cols. Heck and Scott. The Federal troops, through the aid of a Union traitor, managed to cut off Pegram from succor from either party; they heard the roar of battle, but had received no orders to move. Scott, when he saw no chance of succoring Pegram, ordered a retreat, which was effected in good order to Greenbriar river. Col. Heck made his way through the mountain passes and joined Garnett's forces, which were at Laurel Hill. Nearly all of Capt. Irvin's company, from Buckingham,

McClellan led the proud invading host,
While Garnett on the hill-slope took his post,
Cheer'd his worn men and bade them not forget
Their peaceful homes by hireling bands beset:
  Upon Rich Mountain noble Pegram stood
Behind his new-made works of earth and wood;
The Fed'rals charged—the Spartan band gave way,
Their leader fell the foremost in the fray.
Then turned the tide of fight to Laurel Hill,
Where Garnett's forces stood like statues still;
Four times their number press'd upon their flanks,
And every volley thinn'd their pent-up ranks.
Their luckless chief with firmness stood the shock,
Which surging came, like waves against a rock;
"Be firm, my boys, aim low," brave Garnett cried—
A ball sped thro' the air—he fell and died!

---

were killed, together with all the officers, with the exception of Lieut.
Colonel Bondurant. The Southern loss was 75 killed and about as
many wounded. The Federal loss was 11 killed and 35 wounded.

Gen. Garnett, on learning of the engagement, left his entrenched
camp at Huttonville with the main body of his army, leaving what is
supposed to be but a camp guard there. He advanced to succor
Pegram, and had arrived within three miles of Beverly, when he was
met by Pegram's flying forces, who were foremost in the retreat. As
they rushed in among Garnett's troops, they created a panic which
made the General unable to control them; he retreated accordingly in
the direction of St. George's.

McClellan followed up his immense conquest of a handful of Spar-
tans, and marched towards Beverly, encountering Gen. Garnett, with
the main body of Confederates, at Laurel Hill. The overwhelming
numbers of the invading army did not deter the gallant Garnett from
disputing his advance. He formed in line of battle, and poured a raking fire into the enemy's ranks, which was promptly returned. A
charge was made upon his battery, which was feebly resisted by the
Confederates. In a short time the line gave way, and the brave Garnett was struck by a musket ball, and fell dead, while in the act of
attempting to rally his men.

No braver man than he—true to the last;
A hero born—fell'd by misfortune's blast.

But hath the Muse no vict'ry to recount,
No glorious deeds to cause the soul to mount?
Aye—turn we now towards Manassas plains,*
Where gory Havoc all majestic reigns;
Where shouting hosts are charging front to front,
And snorting war-steeds court the battle's brunt;

---

* On the 18th July the grand affair of Manassas opened with a rencontre between the advance guards of the Confederate army under Gens. Beauregard and Johnston, and the invading army under Gen. McDowell. The Southern troops were strongly entrenched at Manassas Junction, and also had advanced batteries along the line of Bull Run, about five miles towards Centreville. The advance guard of the Federals was at the latter place 5,000 strong, our force numbering about 3,000. On the 18th the invaders advanced towards Manassas Junction, and attempted to cross the fords at several points, but were repulsed by the Confederate troops three times, with a heavy loss on their side. At about 5 o'clock in the afternoon they retreated in great confusion, two of our regiments pursuing them. A large number were taken prisoners. The casualties on the Confederate side were few.

The pursuing regiments, finding a large force at Fairfax C. H., after exchanging a few shots, returned to Bull Run, Gen. Beauregard preferring to give them battle there. The General was hurriedly sent for, and quickly came to the scene of action, when he ordered a retreat, which proved to be a brilliant strategic movement. At first the troops murmured, but when they heard that it was Beauregard's wish, they were perfectly satisfied.

The regiments engaged in this brilliant affair were the First Virginia, Col. Moore, the Seventeenth (Alexandria), the Mississippi and the Louisiana. The enemy outnumbered them in proportion of three to one. The Washington Artillery, of New Orleans, were in the early stage of the action. Col. Moore was wounded. Capt. James K. Lee and Lieut. H. H. Miles were killed. The enemy's loss about 500—ours 152 killed, wounded and missing. Two cannon and 500 stand of arms were taken from the enemy.

This brilliant affair (sometimes called the battle of Bull Run) was the prelude to the grand battle, which took place on Sunday, 21st, two days after.

Full of hope and emblazoned with arrogance, notwithstanding his numerous defeats, Gen. Scott, urged, it was said, by barking politicians

Where Beauregard and Johnston lead our arms,
And guide the lightning of the warring storms;
Where Davis stands all fearless on the field,
Quick to command, as quick the sword to wield.

Record, O Muse! that wild, that fearful strife,
Where clashing hosts with bayonet and knife
Prey'd on each other—spurred the fiery steed,
And laugh'd to see their dying *kinsmen* bleed.
Tell of the havoc of Confederate guns—
The shameful flight of Northern myrmidons;
Tell of the flash of bayonet and sword,
Tell of the brave, the peerless Beauregard.

---

and editors, yielded to the cry of "ONWARD TO RICHMOND!" and ordered Gen. McDowell to scatter Beauregard's forces to the four winds of heaven. Months of preparation had completed his "Grand Army," and placed them upon a *war footing.* The word went forth from Washington "Advance!"—and advance it was. The night before the expected victory, hosts of functionaries, congressmen, editors, reporters and civilians rushed to witness the expected *victory.* Aye, even the *ladies* so far forgot themselves as to join the gay party, and *feast* their vision on ghastly corpses, broken limbs, and the unnatural struggle of brother against brother and father against son. So sure were the invaders of victory, that they brought rich viands, wines and cigars with them for a merry feast on the field of blood and carnage!

Gens. Johnston and Patterson had for some days previous been playing a game of chess between Winchester, which was occupied by the former, and Martinsburg, the quarters of the latter. Patterson, tired of Johnston's by-play, made a retrograde towards the Potomac, probably with the intention of joining McDowell, though he did not. The cunning Johnston, suspecting this, made a forced march, and on the evening of the 20th was by the side of Beauregard, while the Pennsylvania commander was—nowhere.

There are numerous accounts of this severe conflict,—all of them differ. Those of the northern journals, however graphic they may be, are tinged with that illiberality which, during the entire war, characterized the Republican press. Those of the southern journals were carried away by enthusiasm and a warm, patriotic desire to let the world know what could be done by men fighting for their homes and those they loved best.

Red dawn stole up the cloudless eastern sky
In lambent rays; the pale stars shrunk away,
Until our eagle with unblinking eye
Gazed on the glowing face of th' god of day.
The mountain peaks were bright with morning's beam,
The forest warblers sang their matin song;
And gladly sparkled every valley stream,
Cheering the soldier as he march'd along.
Far off the foe, with steady tramp, advanc'd,
Their bayonets glitt'ring in the golden light;
While round our banners amorous breezes danc'd,
And brave men rallied for the coming fight.
On, on, true hearts! a foe pollutes your soil,
The welkin rings with shouts of scorn and ire;

President Davis was on the field, and aided Beauregard and Johuston in their grand work.

History will give the details of this great victory for the young republic—my limits will not allow me to enter into them; the dispatch of President Davis sums up all. "The enemy was routed, and fled precipitately, abandoning a very large amount of arms, munitions, knapsacks and baggage. The ground was strewn with those killed for miles, and the farm houses and grounds around were filled with his wounded. The pursuit was continued along several routes towards Leesburg and Centreville, until darkness covered the fugitives. We have captured several field batteries and regimental standards, and one United States flag. Many prisoners have been taken. Too high praise cannot be bestowed, whether for the skill of the principal officers or the gallantry of all the troops. The battle was warmly fought on our left, several miles from our field works; our force engaged there not exceeding fifteen thousand—that of the enemy estimated at thirty-five thousand."

In this severe battle the losses of both sides were as follows:

	Confederates.	Federals.
Killed	393	1,000
Wounded	1,200	2,500
Prisoners	50	1,000
	1,643	4,500

Crush the vile serpent in his deadly coil,
  Consume him with a blast of lead and fire.
On speeds the stalwart Texan—eagle-eyed,
  His faithful rifle takes its deadly poise;
While Georgia's nobles, charging side by side,
  Shout their war-song above the conflict's noise.
Wild on the left the crash of arms is heard,
  · The iron dogs belch out their streams of fire;
But Johnston's there—he gives the cheering word,
  And shouting ranks press on with mighty ire.
No kindly dews of Heav'n come down to cool
  The parched lip or damp the burning head;
The sun looks down on many a bloody pool,
  Where prostrate lies the gallant Southron—dead.
Virginia—mother—see thy dauntless sons,
  Robed in the smoke of booming cannonry,
While whistling balls from Mississippi's guns
  Reach hearts that throbb'd to crush the brave and free.
Then the old line of groaning Maryland,
  · With piercing cry, still writhing in their chains,
Plunge in the fight with reeking sword in hand,
  Strewing the foemen's dead along the plains.
The old North legions wake the echo's song,
  The proud Palmetto sign 'mid dun clouds soars;
While Alabama's hosts rush fast along,
  And struggle where the wildest tumult roars.
Lo! Louisiana's sons, with brawny arm,
  Their brazen war-dogs wield; while Tennessee
Rolls in her cohorts—like a howling storm
  Blasting the foe with lightning of the free.

With glittering knife, the men of Arkansas
  Plunge madly thro' the ranks of shrieking foes;
In vain they plead—their day of triumph's o'er,
  And Vengeance laughs above their dying throes.
That long, that weary day! that day of strife!
  How blush'd the sun as wearily he set!
He rose—and smiled on many a cherished life,
  He sank—and left the field with life-tide wet.
The proud battalions of the Northern host
  Falter—they yield, and soon are scatter'd wide;
Spur your fleet steeds! or half the vict'ry's lost,
  And strew their bodies on the highway side.
Now faint and fainter hums the din of war,
  Night throws her veil around the scene of blood;
Tears sparkle in the blink of every star,
  The pensive moon draws round her misty hood.
But Hist'ry's page in words of light shall tell
  How nobly Southern patriots fought and bled;
The poet's harp a hymn of praise shall swell,
  A mourning nation bless the hallow'd dead.

Muffle the harp strings, let the requiem swell,
Wreathe laurel round the tombs of those who fell;
Weep for the dead—the honor'd dead, who stood
The fleshwalls of their homes 'mid fire and blood.
The dauntless Bee, who charged the staggering foe,
The gallant Fisher, Thomas and Bartow;
Hale, Daniel, Radford—Miles and gentle Lee,
Dying to live fresh in our memory.
They fell as heroes ever wish to fall,
The turf their bier—the smoke their funeral pall.

5

At Carthage Seigel's Hessians were assail'd
By State rights troops, and 'neath their valor quail'd;*
Routed by Jackson, ere McCulloch's force
Could reach the scene, they fled both man and horse,
Leaving the dead and wounded on the plain,
Their standard fallen—never to float again.
Onward to Springfield sped the scatter'd host,
With all their stores and ammunition lost.
Lyon receiv'd them—rallied their broken ranks,
And sallied forth to check McCulloch's pranks,
Who, with his border men, was marching down
With fire and sword upon the fated town.

With early morn the sanguine fight begun,†
The heavy clouds had pass'd, the golden sun
Shone on the hostile armies in array,
Their bayonets glistening in the beams of day.

---

* The State troops, under Gov. Jackson, of Missouri, met the Union
forces, under Col. Seigel, unexpectedly, at about eight miles north of
Carthage. They were 2,500 strong, and having the choice of ground,
had planted their cannon in the most commanding position. Gov.
Jackson had about 12,000 men, of whom only about 2,000 were armed,
except with shot guns. He however gave Seigel battle for eight hours,
and finally routed him, capturing 700 prisoners, four cannon, and a
great amount of army supplies, &c. Ben McCulloch came to Jackson's
aid, but too late for service on that field. Following up the foe, he
brought on the severe battle of Springfield.

† The battle of Springfield, Mo., took place on the 10th of August.
The Federal forces, under Gen. Lyon, left the town, where they quar-
tered, for the purpose of attacking the Missourians, under Gen. Ben
McCulloch. There were many conflicting accounts as to the result of
this battle, both in the northern and southern journals. McCulloch calls
it *Oak Hills* in his official report, and says that his effective force was
5,300 infantry, 15 pieces of artillery, and 6,000 horsemen, armed with
flint-lock muskets, rifles and shot guns. Gen. Lyon attacked him on
the left, and Gen. Seigel on the right. The conflict was long and bloody,
and the Federals lost many of their best officers, among them Gen.

Brave Lyon led the well-arm'd Federals on,
By firm Missouri troops the shock was borne,
A murd'rous volley fired—then soon return'd, .
Till ranks gave way, and hearts with vengeance burn'd.
Proud Lyon fell—mourn'd by his robber band,
The bravest Northern chief—born to command.

Then chang'd the conflict from the right and left
Upon the centre, which was quickly cleft;
The brave Missourians, Price's chosen boys, .
·With shot-guns, rifles, knives and other *toys*,
Rush'd in pell-mell with loud and piercing whoop,
Back'd by the Louisiana and Arkansas troop.
The Union ranks give way—they yield—they fly,
The Patriot cause gains one more victory! ·
But, oh! how dearly won. Brave Weightman fell,
And Hinson, Alexander, Brown and Bell,
Walton and Weaver—brave, unflinching men,
Honor'd in song and named by History's pen.

Relentless War! cannot thy fearful rage
    Be pent in battle field or on the deep?
Why on the innocent thine anger wage,
    Leaving the old and young to wail and weep.
Let man meet man with weapon sharp and keen,
    Grapple for life upon the warlike plain;

Lyon, who fell early in the day. The Confederates also met with severe loss among their officers. Gens. Slack and Clarke were severely wounded, Gen. Price slightly. Col. Weightman was killed, also Lt. Col. Austin, Col. B. J. Brown, Capts. Blackwood, Enyard, and Lieut. Hughes. It was a great victory of the troops of Missouri and Arkansas, who took 400 prisoners, several stand of colors, and a large quantity of good arms. Our killed amounted to 265, wounded 800, missing 30.

The quiet home should never be the scene
　Of deadly strife—there Peace should ever reign.
Hampton, thou fairest village of the shore!*
Where old elms cast their shadows on each door,
Where quiet reign'd, ere War's shrill clarion rung,
Where rustic beauty smiled and poets.sung;
Where all thy beauty now?　Dark Solitude
Hangs o'er thy ruins, crawling reptiles brood
Where prattling children gambol'd joyous, free,
And blacken'd walls are all that's left of thee!

　Well I remember many a pleasant day
Pass'd with dear friends—now scatter'd far away,
Whose hearts were in their hands—who sipp'd
Sweets from the flow'r before its leaves were stripp'd.

　How points the hand of time on yonder tower?
Close on the noon of night; the stilly hour
When motley forms creep thro' the sleeper's brain,
And Chanticleer sends forth his clarion strain.
Myriads of stars wink in their azure spheres,
And fashion music, strange to earthly ears,

---

* On the morning of the 8th August the Confederate forces under
Gen. Magruder, whose camp was at Yorktown, marched towards
Hampton, then occupied by Gen. Butler's Federal troops.　He went
within a mile and a half of the town, and halted.　At night large fires
were built at this point, and the General withdrew to within three
miles of Hampton.　After midnight, finding that the enemy made no
demonstration whatever, he despatched some two or three regiments of
infantry and a troop of cavalry into town, with instructions to burn it.
This force entered the town, and with the aid of some of the citizens,
set fire to it at about 3 o'clock in the morning.　By daylight it was
reduced to ashes.　Many of the Confederate officers and privates were
citizens of Hampton, and owners of the property they consumed.　The
burning of the town was considered a military necessity, as it was ascer-
tained that it was to be made the winter quarters of the Federals.

While slowly sinks the silent moon, her beams
Kissing the wavelets of a thousand streams.
'T is the high carnival of thought, when Heaven
Seems nearest Earth, and when to man is given
The power to conjure up the dreamy past,
To raise the veil o'er happier moments cast.

Ye chosen few! I see ye mirrored up,
Like roses wreathed around a banquet cup;
I see your smile diffusing joy around,
I hear your laugh, the happy spirit's bound.
Electric sparks play round the lips of Wit,
And fan a flame that man may hallow it,
While wrinkled Care breaks loose his heavy toils,
And reads a lesson in Good Humor's smiles.
How fleetly glided by the sunny hours,
When life was like a pilgrimage o'er flowers.
The air seem'd fill'd with laughing sprites; the sea
Sang its hoarse anthem, wild—yet merrily,
While dancing waves roll'd shouting up the shore,
And clapp'd their hands as playful as of yore.
The woods were eloquent with jovial sounds,
The snort of steeds, the merry cry of hounds,
While from her covert sprang th' affrighted deer,
With lofty bound and eye illum'd by fear.
Each rivulet sang songs of joy, and roll'd
In merry humor o'er its sands of gold;
And e'en the cliffs, whose hoary brows o'erhung
The dark ravine, their mystic pæans sung
With ten-fold wildness, sending back the strain
Which merry voices utter'd on the plain.

When shall we meet again, ye chosen few,
To pluck wild flowers, to sip the honey-dew?
When shall our lips, by kindly words, impart
The healing balm unto the wounded heart?
When silvery tresses wave around the brow,
And hearts are chill'd that pulse so warmly now;
When the frail form, bent down by weight of years,
Halts at the grave, and sprinkles it with tears—
Tears for the one that 's gone before, whose bed
Tells lingering ones the story of the dead.

May Time's hand lightly press upon your brow,
Keep ever bright the smiles so radiant now,
While from his wings falls Pleasure's diamond dew,
To throw life's fragrance round the chosen few.
With blazing brand, War laid thy houses low,
  The tower'd church, the school-house and the cot;
The grand old trees shrunk in the with'ring glow,
  And vine and rose-bush crimp'd and fell—to rot.
The foeman now treads o'er thy crumbling walls,
The owlets roost within thy silent halls;
And in the grave-yard, where our loved ones sleep,
Rude enemies their noisy revels keep.*

---

 *There was an old Episcopal Church in Hampton, one of the oldest
in the Southern Confederacy. It was not fired by the troops, but
caught from the other buildings. The vandals of Butler's army dese-
crated the hallowed grave-yard where lay the remains of the ancestors
of many an honorable Virginia family. They cooked their meats on the
venerated slabs that recorded the names of the departed—played cards
and frolicked away the time under the shade of the revered old trees.
  The writer of this poem cherishes many sweet memories of the
town of Hampton—he resided there, formed many lasting attachments,
and the remains of his beloved partner lie sleeping there. His rhap-
sody will therefore be excused by the generous reader.

Sweet, peaceful Hampton—now thyself no more—
But a dark monument of blasting War!

Now through the deep a vast armada sped,*
  From old Monroe, with guns of heavy weight,
And armed hosts by brutish Butler led;
  Its aim the seaboard of the old North State.
Fort Clarke first felt the power of its shot,
The battering was quick and short—but hot;
Then Hatteras received the iron shower,
And thunder'd back with all her might and power.
But 't was of no avail, though to the last
The heroes faced the missiles thick and fast;
Yet might prevail'd, the gallant fortress fell,
The victors landed with loud shout and yell.
Thus gain'd the foe a foothold on the coast,
While we eight hundred noble patriots lost.

---

* On the 25th August an extensive expedition was organized, and left Fortress Monroe under command of Gen. Butler. It consisted of the frigates Minnesota and Wabash, the ship-of-war Pawnee, the gunboats Monticello and Harriet Lane, steamers Adelaide and George Peabody, propellers Fanny and Adriatic, with a large number of schooners, barges, &c. The steamer Quaker City followed shortly afterwards. These vessels carried over 100 guns and 4,000 men. Much curiosity and interest were manifested for several days to know where this fleet would turn up.

On the 28th the fleet appeared off the coast of North Carolina. Fort Clarke was first attacked, and the garrison being soon driven out, sought refuge in Fort Hatteras, some two miles further south. The enemy then poured in a shower of shell and round shot upon Hatteras, which our men were unable to return effectually *because their long range guns were not mounted.* The attack was made at 8 o'clock in the morning, and kept up until 11 A. M. the next day. Eleven of the enemy's vessels were engaged in the bombardment. From six to eight hundred prisoners were taken by the enemy, among them Col. Martin and Commodore Barron.

At Cross Lanes vict'ry perch'd upon our flag,*
Her cheering shout was sent from crag to crag.
The patriot Floyd marshall'd our gallant band,
Repell'd the foe while fighting hand to hand.
Many a Hessian fell—the rest took heel,
Awed at the keenness of our Southern steel.
' Again near Summerville Floyd's brave brigade †
Won lasting fame. Behind their palisade
Of earth and logs they gall'd the daring foe,
Scatter'd their legions, laid their proudest low;
Till sick with slaughter, from the field they fled,
With scarcely time to gather in their dead.
Night gather'd round—the foe was reinforc'd
By more than double what their ranks had lost;

---

* On the 26th August an engagement took place at a place called
"Cross Lanes," near the junction of Meadow and Gauley Rivers, some
twenty miles above the mouth of the latter stream, between General
Floyd's forces and 1,300 Federals. The enemy were repulsed in less
than an hour, losing all their wagons and baggage of every description. They also suffered a loss of 50 killed and wounded, and from 60
to 100 prisoners.

† On the 11th September a battle occurred near Summerville, in
Western Virginia. Gen. Rosencranz, after making a reconnoissance,
found Gen. Floyd with his army of 5,000, with 16 field pieces,
entrenched on the top of a mountain on the west side of Gauley River.
The position was guarded by heavy forts and a jungle. The action was
opened by Floyd's Artillery. The enemy was mostly posted in the
road—and some accounts have it that his loss was terrible, while on the
Confederate side only one was killed, one drowned and seven wounded.
Rosencranz made a vigorous attack, driving in the advanced guard and
assailing Floyd in his position a short distance from the North bank
of the Gauley. The enemy was frequently and successfully repulsed,
and, it is said, with a loss of four or five hundred. Gen. Floyd was
slightly wounded ; he crossed the river, and Rosencranz fell back.
Floyd, by this movement, effected a junction with Gen. Wise, on the
Lunday road. This affair is sometimes called the "Battle of Carnefax
Ferry."

Wisely our Gen'ral cross'd the turbid. flood,
And, when the morning broke, the breastworks stood,
But not a soldier for the feast of blood.
Fair Lexington had long in bondage groan'd,*
    The tyrant's chains were closely round her drawn;
Her beauteous daughters wept, her old men moan'd,
    And prayed to Heav'n for Freedom's happy dawn.
Her streets were press'd by armed foreign hordes,
    Her halls of learning turn'd to barrack pens;
And e'en the fanes, held sacred as the Lord's,
    Were chang'd to filthy and unholy dens.
But nobly Price, with soldiers used to war,
Came rushing on like waves upon the shore;
While Rains, with batt'ries thundering fast and loud,
Sent death amid the starving Yankee crowd.
"Water!" they cried—"to wet our parched lips;"†
And from a passing cloud the liquid drips;

---

* On the 16th September a severe siege took place of the town of Lexington, Mo., which lasted from that day to the 21st, on which day Col. Mulligan, with 3,500 Federal troops, surrendered to the Confederate forces under Gen. Price. According to the Northern accounts Mulligan's reinforcements were intercepted and driven back. The situation of his men grew desperate, sorties and skirmishes took place constantly. The Home Guard became disaffected and first raised the white flag. Finally the Federal officers held a council and decided to capitulate. Price demanded the unconditional surrender of the officers; the men were allowed to depart without arms, after taking an oath not to fight in future against the Confederate States. A large quantity of specie and other property were captured. After the surrender of Lexington, Gov. Jackson with the Legislature assembled and passed the ordinance of secession. Lexington was made the capital of the State of Missouri.

† At the siege of Lexington, the inhabitants were cut off from the river, and no water was to. be obtained. Rain at intervals came to gratify their thirst; instances occurred where soldiers spread out their blankets until thoroughly wet. and then wrung them into their camp dishes, carefully saving the priceless fluid thus obtained.

6

No river, gurgling fount or stagnant pool
Quench'd their mad thirst or made their foreheads cool.
For five long, weary days the siege held out,
And shot and shell flew fearfully about,
Till disaffection crept from man to man,
And mutiny its secret work began.
The white flag wav'd—then Mercy took her throne,
The huge siege-guns then hush'd their thundering tone.
The town was freed—the stars and bars were hail'd,
Once more the tyrant 'neath their beauty quail'd.
High on Cheat Mountain stood the haughty foe,*

   Entrench'd around with rows of bristling guns;
Jackson, the dauntless hero, stood below,

   His men array'd where clear Greenbriar runs.
He challenged forth th' invaders of his home,
And bid them from their strong entrenchments come,
And give him fight; this banter Reynolds took,
And down he came from stony peak and nook.

   The sun was up, his mild October rays
Glanc'd o'er the woods and fields of yellow maize,
When, suddenly, the pickets left their posts,
And hurried in before th' advancing hosts.
Soon down the slope a rattling volley pour'd,
'Twas answered quick while loud artillery roar'd.

---

*On the 13th October the Federal army under Gen. Reynolds attacked the Confederate forces under Gen. H. R. Jackson at Greenbriar river. The enemy had been strongly entrenched and fortified on the top of Cheat Mountain, and our troops considering it hopeless to attack such a position, tried every means to get them out. At daylight on the 13th, Reynolds came down with 5,000 men, and drove in the Confederate pickets. The battle then commenced and raged four and a half hours, when the enemy retreated with a reported loss of 1,500 killed and wounded. The Confederate loss was seven killed, twenty wounded and twelve missing.

With steady aim brave Shumaker threw out
His iron messengers, which flew about
So swift and fast, that columns strong gave way,
And hundreds kiss'd the sod that noisy day.

In the reserve a vet'ran soldier stood
Upon his rifle leaning, in a mood
That seem'd like revery. He watch'd the fight,
And, when the cannon peal'd, his eyes would light,
His bosom swell—his lips give out " hurra! "
So proud was he of carnage and of war.
A rifle's crack was heard—down fell a foe ;
"Ah, ha!" shriek'd he with joy, "that's our Joe;
I know his *critter's* voice—she's quick and true,
And Joe's the boy for Yankee-doodle-doo."
Another crack from the thick brush below,
Again he bellow'd out, "that's our Joe!"
At length a cannon spoke in awful tones,
And sent its deadly ball thro' flesh and bones ;
Up leapt the old man, with a Hoosier crow,
Shouting above the din, "that's our Joe!"

But sorrow came to that gray-bearded man,
Whose years of life were but a narrow span.
They brought a dead youth from the bloody plain,
And said a bullet had gone through his brain ;
The old man groan'd in agony of woe,
And gazing on his son, sighed, *"that's our Joe!"*
For hours they fought, but Jackson held his ground;

It was high noon, when, yielding to the shock,
The Northmen on their heels turn'd quick around,
And left our heroes firm as Otter's rock.

Hundreds there lay upon the stubble plain,
Never to raise their battle cry again.

At Santa Rosa's isle our stalwart men *
  Cross'd o'er the bay and storm'd the foeman's camp;
Led on by Anderson thro' sand and fen,
  Thro' fields of cane and many a gloomy swamp.
Wilson's Zouaves—the pick'd of New York's scum,
Lay quarter'd there, and hush'd was fife and drum;
They soundly slept, when rattling muskets told
That some strange foe was there—supremely bold.
Faintly resisting—then, all *sans culotte*,
They ran and made good time while dodging shot;
Many fell, grov'ling in the sand—our men
Laid waste their camp, and then went back again.
  And then, at Barboursville†—near Leesburg too,‡
Great deeds were done by Southrons brave and true;

---

* On the night of the 10th October, Santa Rosa Island, near Pensacola, was stormed by the Confederate troops, 1,000 in number, under Gen. Anderson, and the Federal camp broken up. This camp was occupied by the celebrated Billy Wilson's Zouaves. They burnt and destroyed every building (except the hospital), with immense quantities of rations, equipments, stores and munitions. All the cannon were spiked. Loss of the enemy very great—that of the Confederates was 40 killed and wounded. One account states that Billy Wilson made his escape to Fort Pickens *sans culotte.*

†On the 14th October a brilliant affair took place at Barboursville, Ky., Cols. Rains and Brunner started on a scouting expedition, taking 26 men with them. Near Barboursville they were fired on by the Federals in ambush; they routed the enemy, and returned to camp, giving the alarm. Col. Battle assembled a force, and made after the enemy, who was reported at Barboursville. A brisk firing commenced near the town—a gallant charge was made by our troops, the Federals fled, leaving nineteen dead on the field, besides arms, ammunition and two prisoners. Lieut. Powell, of Cummings' regiment, was killed.

‡ On the 18th of October, Capt. Ashby's cavalry engaged a detachment of the enemy between Leesburg and Harper's Ferry, Va., and

While Hollins' fleet at Mississippi's mouth,
Scatter'd their ships—the torments of the South.*
On old Potomac's rocky banks there stood
An armed host, thirsting for Southern blood;
Their weapons glitter'd in the setting sun,
Which linger'd in the west, as they begun
To cross the stream and climb the rugged way
That led to Leesburg, where our forces lay.†
The Mississippi boys were sent to meet
This hostile band. Right bravely did they greet
The proud invader—every volley's roar
Waked doubling echoes on the craggy shore.

---

badly routed them. Federal loss 16 killed and 15 wounded; the Confederate loss one killed and one wounded.

* On the 12th October a spirited naval exploit took place at the head of the passes in the mouth of the Mississippi River. It seems that Commodore Hollins, of the C. S. Navy, conceived the idea of *breaking the blockade* by scattering the Federal ships off New Orleans. He succeeded, after a very short struggle, in driving them aground—one of them was sunk. The attempt was brilliant, but accomplished no good.

† The sanguinary battle of Leesburg took place near that town on the 21st October. The details of the Northern journals were truly sickening, and it was pronounced more bloody, in proportion, than the fierce conflict at Bull Run. On Sunday, the 20th, the Confederate troops were prepared for hot work, Gen. Evans having received information that the enemy were crossing the river. On Monday, about 8 o'clock, the battle commenced with a roar of artillery, which was the signal for the opening of one of the severest fights of the war. The enemy were frequently repulsed with great slaughter, leaving their dead and mangled bodies strewn over the ground like autumn leaves; and, in their precipitate retreat, it is estimated that more than one hundred found a watery grave, while no less than 657 were made prisoners. Gen. Stone commanded the Federals, amounting to about 2,000, the advance of Gen. Banks' army—their total loss was estimated at from 1,000 to 1,200; among their killed was Col. Baker, ex-United States Senator. Our entire loss in killed and wounded was 159, among the former was Col. Burt, of the 18th Mississippi regiment, a brave and accomplished soldier.

Then forward sprang from ambush dark and deep
Virginia's Eighth—in companies they sweep
The open field amid the galling fire   •
Of twice their force—compass'd by slaughter dire.
The men of Mississippi then fell in,
Blending their war-cry with the musket's din,
Captured the Yankee guns with shout and yell,
Nor ceas'd their work till haughty Baker fell.
Down the sharp crags that hung above the shore,
The Yankees leapt, all weltering in their gore,
Then, battling with the waves, they scream'd in vain
For help—they sank—never to rise again.
Honor to Evans and his brave brigade!
Who gave th' invader soil—but with a spade.
Tears for the gallant Burt, who nobly fell
Beneath the flag he loved so long and well.

Thus far our cause had prosper'd, but reverse
    Will sometimes throw its sombre shadow far;
Let the sad Muse the dark tale now rehearse,
    'Tis hers—the task to sing of fickle War.
Port Royal fell 'mid storms of deadly hail,*
And peal on peal that made the stoutest quail;

---

* On the 6th November the vast armada, so long fitting out by the
Federal Government, having reached its destination, made a descent
upon Port Royal, on the coast of South Carolina.   The assault of this
huge armament was gallantly resisted by the Confederate gunners, but
overcome by a largely superior force, the forts were compelled to yield.
The battle commenced at between 8 and 9 o'clock, A. M., by the fleet
advancing into the harbor in single file, headed by the flag-ship Minnesota, under Commodore Dupont, which was followed by some twelve or
thirteen propellers of great power, most of which had sailing frigates in
tow.   The Forts Walker and Beauregard opened upon them, which

In vain her brave defenders plied their guns,
In vain the Georgians, Carolina's sons
And German gunners, sent the thunders back,
The Yankee fleet kept on their watery track,
Veer'd and spit out their streams of flame and smoke,
Till the calm waters from their slumbers broke,
And froth capp'd waves danc'd up toward the sky,
Lash'd by the balls in their mad revelry.
Port Royal fell! its forts and harbor fair—
A foreign standard now is waving there.

At Belmont Havoc raised his piercing yell,*
  Let loose his furies 'mid the struggling bands;
While May at Piketon on the foemen fell,†
  And dug their graves with eager, bloody hands.

---

was replied to by broadsides from the frigates. For a long time the combat was terrific, guns of the heaviest calibre being used. Our forts fired several of their ships, but the flames were quickly extinguished. At about 3 o'clock but three of the guns of Fort Walker remained in position. Our men, especially the German Artillery, behaved with great coolness and bravery. Our loss at Fort Walker was supposed to be about 100 in killed and wounded, of which the German Artillery lost eight killed and fourteen wounded. The garrison were compelled to evacuate the position and retreat to Bluffton. Sometime after the Hilton Head battery had to be yielded, that of Bay Point was also left by our troops, who fell back on St. Helena and Beaufort.

* On the 7th November a glorous victory was achieved by the Confederate troops at Belmont, Ky. The fight commenced at 11 o'clock in the morning, and lasted until 5 o'clock in the evening. The northern and southern accounts of this battle are very conflicting. The loss of the Confederates is estimated at 585, killed, wounded and missing, that of the Federals at 548. The Confederates fairly claim a brilliant victory, as the enemy left the field and retreated across the river.

† On the 8th November a severe conflict between the Confederate and Federal forces occurred near Piketon, Ky. . It took place a few miles beyond Piketon, on the Louisa River, just west of the mouth of Ivy Creek, which empties into the Louisa from the north side. The road beyond the river from the mouth of the Ivy is over a steep bluff,

At Alleghany, where bold Johnson's force *
Was camp'd, the foe with infantry and horse
Made fight, but dearly rued the fearful hour
They came to test the dauntless Southron's power.
And then again at Dranesville freely flow'd †
The tide of life, and Death's cold, shadowy abode

---

rising thirty feet perpendicularly from the water. Along the side of
the road for four or five hundred yards west of the mouth of the Ivy,
which is spanned by a high bridge, the mountain rises to a great height
by a very precipitous ascent, thickly covered with ivy, laurel, and other
evergreens. Into this covert, along the steep ascent, Capt. Jack May
placed his sharp-shooters, about 300 in number, a short time before the
advance column of the enemy came up. He then set fire to the bridge.
The enemy's advance soon appeared, suspecting nothing; and, seeing
the bridge on fire, supposed that our force had retreated to the other
side. When four or five hundred yards of the road below him was
filled with men, crack went the rifles of Jack May and his sharp shoot-
ers along the whole distance. They continued to load and fire for several rounds, and then, at a signal, they vanished around the mountain,
and up Ivy Creek to a temporary crossing, which they had taken care
to provide, and which they destroyed after they had crossed the river.

May lost two of his men killed, and fifteen wounded. The dead of
the enemy were piled in heaps in the road. Between five and six hundred is said to have been the loss of the enemy. May found his way
safely back to the camp of Col. Williams.

* On the morning of the 12th December a severe battle was fought
near the foot of Alleghany mountain, in Western Virginia. The action
was commenced on the evening of the 11th, and renewed on the morning of the 12th. The Federals, who were doubtless guided by Union
men in the vicinity, came upon the Confederates under Col. Johnson,
soon after daylight, from the North, their strength being four regiments
of about 1,000 men each; our force consisted of three regiments of an
average of 400 each, two battalions numbering together 200 men, and
two batteries of four guns each. The fight continued until 2 o'clock,
P. M., when the enemy retreated. Capts. Anderson, of the Lee Battery, and Mayneham were killed. In this battle it is said that Col.
Johnson "covered himself with glory."

† On the 20th December a severe fight took place at Dranesville,
Va., which resulted badly to the Confederates, though it was pronounced a "drawn battle." The patriots of the South had to contend
against fearful odds. Gen. Stuart commanded the Confederate forces.
Lt. Col. Martin was killed in the action.

Was fill'd with flesh and bones.   Here Martin fell
His pall the smoke—the cannon's roar his knell.
At Somerset, brave Zollicoffer died,*
A son of Tennessee—his army's pride.
It was a fearful fight—the Spartan bands
Roll'd on the turf with cold and bloody hands;
They fought 'gainst odds and firmly stood the brunt,
Young Bailie Peyton perish'd in the front.

Gloom after gloom! the Southern star shone dim,
   Crush'd, but not conquer'd, were our warriors bold;
Great God is just, they placed their faith in him,
   And still fought on beneath their banner's fold.
Off Roanoke a line of gunboats loom'd †
   Above the misty horizon; they seem'd

---

* The battle of Somerset (sometimes called Mill Spring), Ky., occurred on the 19th January, 1862. It was a hard fought conflict, in which our troops signalized themselves in the firm stand they took against the invaders. The Confederate force was under the immediate command of Maj. Gen. Crittenden. Of the death of Gen. Zollicoffer, a writer gives the following particulars: "The Mississippi regiment was ordered to the right, and Battle's to the left, and immediately afterwards, riding up in front, Gen. Zollicoffer advanced to within a short distance of an Ohio regiment, which had taken a position at a point unknown to him, and which he supposed to be one of his regiments. The first intimation he had of his position was received when too late. "There's old Zollicoffer," cried out several of the regiment in front of him, "kill him!" and in an instant their pieces were leveled at his person. At that moment his aid drew his revolver and fired, killing the individual who first recognized Gen. Z. With the most perfect coolness the General approached to the head of the enemy, and drawing his sabre, cut the head of the Lincoln Colonel from his shoulders. As soon as this was done, twenty bullets pierced the body of our gallant leader, and he fell from his horse a mangled corpse."

After suffering severely, our troops, by order of Gen. Crittenden, retreated to their entrenchments.

† The next reverse was that of Roanoke Island, in which, besides a number of brave fellows, Capt. O. Jennings Wise, the son of General

Like huge sea monsters, when their cannon boom'd
  Old Ocean shook—the gull and curlew scream'd.
'Twas Burnside's fleet feeling their doubtful way
Around the isle where our doom'd squadron lay.
Slowly they came where Lynch's ships were moor'd,
And oped their ports—a stream of flame was pour'd
Upon our slender craft, who soon sent back
An iron shower that made their timbers crack.
All day the sun look'd on that stubborn fight,
And silence only came with sable night.
  When morning dawn'd the guns again awoke,
The forts and boats belch'd out their fire and smoke,
While on the land the hostile troops closed in,
Their rattling muskets joining in the din.
The gallant Wise fell crown'd with glory's bays,
Belov'd by all—no tongue but spoke his praise.
And Coles and Selden, likewise brave Monroe;
Firm to the last, they scorn'd the conquering foe.
Our boats gave up—unequal was the fight,
  Our forts were hush'd—'t were madness to reply;
Our troops surrender'd to superior might,
  And darkness brooded o'er our destiny.

Wise, lost his life. The battle of Roanoke Island took place on the
7th and 8th February. The Federal forces and fleet were under Gen.
Burnside, and the Confederates under Gen. Wise. The naval conflict
was short and active. Com. Lynch, who commanded, was badly
wounded and taken prisoner. Three of our gunboats were saved, but
the loss of life was great. It was stated that our loss in killed, wounded
and prisoners was 1,700. About 400 escaped from the Island. The
Federals landed at two points, and at one of the points they waded up
to their waists to effect a landing. Among the officers killed, besides
Capt. Wise, were Capt. Coles, 46th Virginia, Lieut. Selden, C. S. A.,
and Lieut. Neill T. Monroe, 8th North Carolina.

Out in the West reverses follow'd fast,
Fort Henry yielded to the fiery blast;*

---

* The capture of Fort Henry by the combined efforts of the Federal army and gunboats, was the prelude to the surrender of Fort Donelson, which battle lasted through the 13th, 14th, and 15th February; on the 16th the Fort yielded.

Our troops numbered about 18,000, and were under the command of Generals Floyd, Pillow, Buckner, and Bushrod R. Johnson. Most of the regiments were from Tennessee and Mississippi, but Virginia, Alabama, Texas and Arkansas also contributed their quota, and swelled the dimensions of the army to the size named. Active hostilities commenced early in the morning of the first day, but were confined to the outposts and pickets. The next morning our artillery opened upon the enemy, and met with a ready reply; the artillery duel continued throughout the day. The next day witnessed pretty much the same display, with the exception of an occasional skirmish between the infantry and sharp-shooters of both armies; the gunboats also came up the river and opened a vigorous fire upon Fort Donelson; but after a severe exchanging of shots for several hours, fell back disabled. On Friday, the 15th, the cannonading was more terrible than at any time during the siege. Again the gunboats renewed their attack, and again they were compelled to retire, this time they were placed thoroughly *hors du combat*. The infantry also became warmly engaged. During the fight a desperate charge was made by two Illinois regiments upon the 2d Kentucky and 10th Tennessee, but they were met almost hand to hand, and sent back to their entrenchments, leaving a frightful proportion of their dead and mangled upon the field. The day closed without any practical advantage to either party. The next day was the Rubicon of Fort Donelson. The enemy had received large reinforcements, and now numbered 50,000. Snow lay on the ground to the depth of three inches, and a cold, blinding sleet poured incessantly in the faces of the soldiers. Still our men faltered not—a desperate attack was made upon the right flank of the enemy, under the command of Gen. Grant. Not more than 10,000 of our men were engaged in this movement—but it was successful against triple their number. The struggle now became desperate, and the enemy were routed in every direction, when they were again strengthened by a reinforcement of 30,000 fresh troops encompassing the place and completely surrounding our forces. It was useless to contend against such odds; the Fort and army capitulated to the enemy on their own terms. Floyd and Pillow saved portions of their commands.

The total number of our killed and wounded was estimated at from 2,500 to 3,000, while that of the Federals is said to have been from 4 to 6,000. Among our killed were Lieut. Col. Clough, Texas; Lieut. Col. Robb, Clarksville, Tenn.; Capt. May, Memphis, and Capt. Porter, Nashville.

Then up the sluggish Cumberland came boats
With mighty guns—death in their iron throats,
And hosts of armed men, all bent upon
The glorious capture of Fort Donelson.
Floyd, Pillow, Buckner, Bushrod Johnson too,
Led their brigades the snow-clad meadow through;
Charged boldly up, silenc'd their batteries' roar,
'Mid heaps of dead and reeking pools of gore.
The Fort spoke out—the gunboats shrunk away,
Shatter'd and useless in the dreadful fray—
Three dreary days—the slaughter still went on,
The fourth beheld thy fall—brave Donelson!

   With Donelson fell Nashville.   Tyrant rule *
Hung o'er her citizens—a Lincoln tool,
With pow'r despotic waved the iron rod,
And on the necks of free-born people trod.

   In far New Mexico, 'mid hills and vales,
Young Freedom sang her songs and told her tales
To list'ning ears.   Her flame soon spread around,
And proud hearts bounded at the bugle's sound.
Up rose a band of true and hardy men,
And, rushing from the mountain top and glen,

---

   * Immediately after the surrender of Fort Donelson followed the
capitulation of the city of Nashville. Mayor Cheatham, on the arrival
of the Federal troops in the vicinity of the city, repaired to Edgefield,
where they were encamped, and formally tendered the city with all the
public stores it contained, to the commander of the Federal forces. It
was, perhaps, the first city of such size, and containing so large an
amount of valuable stores, that ever surrendered under similar circumstances, to so inconsiderable a force—only 15 men were sent to take
possession. The inhabitants, however, received the soldiers coldly, and
only two or three Union flags were displayed.

They met the foe upon Valverde's plain *
And told how hard they fought by hundreds slain.
Sibley led on the brave Confederates, ·
And, by his valor, added two new States,
Millions of treasure to the public store—
Unfading laurels steep'd in human gore.

But stars will sometimes peep thro' sombre clouds,
  And sunshine gleam into the prison cell;
The mist that vale and flowery hill-side shrouds,
  Will rise and show more brightly wood and dell.
On Hampton's waters lay the wooden walls
  Of Northern pow'r, securely—as they thought,
Nought broke their quiet save the boatswain's calls,
  The whistling steam-pipe and the engine's snort.
From Norfolk's harbor came a huge machine,†
All noiseless creeping thro' the waters green;

---

* The sanguinary battle of Valverde, New Mexico, took place on the 21st February. Gen. Sibley commanded the Confederate forces, and Gen. Canby the Federal; it resulted in a complete defeat of the latter with great loss. It was a great victory; six thousand eight hundred prisoners were captured, and twenty-five millions worth of property secured to the Southern Confederacy, including the territories of Arizona and New Mexico.

† A brilliant naval affair came off at the mouth of James River, on the 8th March, and temporarily opened the blockade. Two first class frigates, the Cumberland and Congress, were destroyed, and the steamer Minnesota and several smaller Yankee craft disabled. The "sea-monster" Virginia (formerly the United States steam frigate Merrimac) had been for a long while fitting for the expedition at Gosport Navy Yard; and when she crept out of the harbor at Norfolk she struck terror to the blockading squadron of Lincoln. The Virginia was under the command of Capt. Buchanan, who was wounded in the engagement. The loss of life on the side of the enemy was terrific, on our side it was small. The Virginia was assisted in this sparkling affair by the Confederate steamers Patrick Henry and Jamestown, besides two or three smaller vessels. Several prizes were taken from the Yankees. The great batteries at Newport News were silenced. The Virginia offered battle the next day, but had but little to contend with.

'T was the Virginia, all in stout iron cased,
A ram at her prow—timbers tightly braced.
Like a huge tortoise, thro' the briny deep
She made her way a harvest rich to reap.
The Cumberland at anchor lay; her crew
Gazed on the craft—a curious thing to view,
When loudly peal'd the dark intruder's gun,
And with a plunge the dreadful work was done:
Down went the gallant frigate; at mast head
Her flag still flying o'er her buried dead.

Then to the Congress turn'd the floating fort,
Her cannon roar from many a hidden port;
While, bounding harmless from her iron roof
The shot fell thick and fast—but proof
Was she against the wild, unceasing shower,
Unhurt herself—to hurt was all her power.
The air was rent with heavy shot and shell,
The spray dash'd up—the waters rose and fell;
The Congress reel'd, her decks all red with gore,
Striking her flag, she ran into the shore.
Oh, the wild screams of dying men! they rent
The air—the ship she lay a monument,
Till red-hot balls the sea-worn fabric burn'd,
Left nought but ribs—*for Congress had adjourn'd.*

Long raged the fight; the scatter'd Yankee fleet
Kept out of range or order'd quick retreat;
The Monitor essay'd to strike her foe,
She made one plunge, and then thought best to go!
Our gallant fleet retir'd when night came on,
For on that day were fadeless laurels won,

While the whole world proclaim'd an era new,
Lauding Buchanan and his sturdy crew.

The busy Burnside push'd his forces on,
   And captur'd Newbern, in the old North State; *
The forts held out and gave them gun for gun,
   But the town fell—'t was so decreed by fate.
In Elkhorn's fight the fierce McCulloch fell,†
   And McIntosh, the bravest of the braves,
Was stricken low—loud cannon rung their knell,
   And mourning comrades wept above their graves.
Led by Van Dorn, our struggling heroes fought
Like tigers at their lairs—the foemen bought
A meagre vict'ry—on the field were spread
Long lines of wounded and of ghastly dead.

Now turn to Karnstown, where our Jackson met ‡
   The boaster Shields, and left his gory mark;.

---

* On the night of the 13th March about 20,000 Federals, attached to the Burnside expedition, landed with artillery and cavalry near the batteries a short distance from the town of Newbern, N. C.; and began skirmishing with their infantry. Their gunboats, about fifty in number, hauled up within gun-range of the batteries, and opened upon them with eight-inch shell. The fight then became general. We had but 6,000 men in the field and at the batteries—our loss in killed, wounded and prisoners was about 1,000. Col. Campbell and Lieut. Col. Haywood were killed. The forts stood the siege bravely, but were compelled to surrender to superior power ; the town of course capitulated.

† On the night of the 6th March, and during the days of the 7th and 8th, a severe battle took place in Arkansas. By some it was called the battle of Sugar Creek, and by others the battle of Elkhorn. The loss was severe on both sides, and the result of little advantage to either. Gen. Van Dorn was in command. The enemy's force amounted to 20,000. Gens. McCulloch and McIntosh, and Col. Herbert were killed, Gens. Price and Slack wounded.

‡ On the 22d and 23d March, a severe encounter took place, between the Confederate forces under " Stonewall " Jackson, and the

Hard was the fight, till Sol in sorrow set,
  And night spread o'er the field her mantle dark.
With foot to foot and eye to eye they strove,
Their wild shout echoing thro' glen and grove;
At night they slept, when broke another day,
The dead lie there—but Jackson was away.

As gentle Spring spread out her feast of flowers,
And kiss'd young buds with pleasant winds and showers,
War frolick'd in his might and flar'd his brand
Over the fields and cities of the land.
In the far West, down in the sunny South,
Vengeance leapt from the cannon's fiery mouth;
The tyrant's yoke upon the true was plac'd,
And Vandal acts made conquerors disgraced.
St. Augustine bow'd to the tyrant's thrall,*
The Mississippi islands, one and all,†

Federals, under Gen. Shields, near Winchester, Va. It is generally
called the battle of Karnstown, and resulted to the advantage of the
Federals, though they were severely dealt with by the Confederates,
who afterwards retreated towards Strasburg. The engagement was
brought on by the gallant Col. Ashby, who always fought the enemy
whenever he showed himself; it commenced about 4 o'clock and ter-
minated when night closed upon the scene of conflict. Both parties
retired from the battle field. Our loss was not over 50 killed and 150
wounded, while that of the enemy was about three times that number.

  * The Federals, leaving their gunboats outside the bar of St. Augustine, Florida, approached the city in a barge, about 40 in number, with
a flag of truce and the American ensign flying. The surrender of the
city and the keys of the Fort were demanded, with the notice that in
the event of a refusal the vessels outside would proceed to shell them.
The City Council was immediately convened, and, after deliberation,
the keys were delivered to the Federal officer in command of the barge.

  † During the month of March and a great part of April, the
invaders of Southern soil slowly but surely converged their forces
towards the centre. Various small battles and skirmishes took place

Yielded 'mid fire and smoke to stronger power,
While Freedom wept away the gloomy hour.
Old Fred'ricksburg, tho' filled with patriots true,*
Besieged and and threaten'd by the hireling crew,
Surrender'd her rights and wore the galling chain,
Praying ere long to breathe free air again.

Not always with the strong will be the race.
There yet were honors for the Southern arms;
For Beauregard still proudly held his place,
The stern director of the battle's storms.
On Shiloh's plains the hostile armies met,†
No earthy fort—no ditch—no parapet;

---

on the banks of the Western rivers and on the coast, their gigantic fleets of gunboats and transports laying desolate the towns and country within the range of their guns. Island No. 10, a strong position on the Mississippi, occupied by the Confederates, after a long and vigorous resistance, surrendered to the enemy.

* In April the city of Fredericksburg, Va., fell into the hands of the enemy, who took possession of the opposite heights, while our troops fell back toward Gordonsville.

† The great encounter at Shiloh, equaled only by the battle of Manassas, somewhat enlivened the drooping spirits of the Southern people. It came off on the 6th and 7th of April. Among the many brave chiefs killed on our side, we have to record the name of Gen. Albert Sidney Johnston, a most accomplished officer and brave soldier. This event gave the command of the Confederate army to Gen. Beauregard, who planned the attack with his usual ability. The Southern and Northern accounts of this affair differ materially; and it is difficult to glean from the mass a reliable detail.

The fight of the first day commenced with heavy skirmishing. Gen. Hardee made the advance upon the enemy's camp, taking him completely by surprise. Gen. Bragg commanded the centre and Gen. Polk the right wing of the army. During the first day the enemy made a great many stands, but in every instance his ranks were broken and disorganized, and occasionally the retreat was very wild and disorderly, the troops breaking to run. The action continued until 6 o'clock in the evening. After having driven the enemy to the range of their

An open field skirted by pine and oak,
That echoed back the sabre's sparkling stroke.
Hardee began the fight—his squadrons' charge,
Like knights of old with battle-axe and targe,
Struck terror to the foe—they waver'd—broke—
And though their guns in tones of anger spoke,
Yet, such a charge! their forward lines gave way
To clattering hoofs and steel that flash'd in day.
Then Bragg and Polk their cohorts hurried fast,
Rolling along, like clouds before the blast,
They plung'd into the fight; the rallied foe
Meeting their charge and dealing blow for blow.

gunboats, our forces abandoned the pursuit, having possession of their
entire camp, stores, &c.   Our force in this engagement did not exceed
30,000; that of the enemy could not have been less than 70,000, under
the command of Gen. Grant, the victor of Donelson.

The next morning, soon after sunrise, the enemy having been heavily
reinforced, made an attempt to force our position.   His attack was
spirited, and the day's fighting was far more severe than that of the
previous day, he being aided by new men from Gen. Buell's command.
Gen. Beauregard was compelled to order his troops to fall back, and in
so doing, for want of transportation, we were compelled to abandon
much of our spoil and of the substantial fruits of our victory, saving
only fourteen cannon.

The events of both days were considered a thorough victory.   It
was simply impossible to essay more than what had already been accomplished by our army, to drive the enemy to the river.

The personal conduct of our Generals in this battle was beyond
all praise.   Gen. Johnston fell gloriously on the field, leading a command in the thickest of the fight.   Gen. Beauregard; covered with
dust and perspiration, never ceased to lead in person and address words
of encouragement to his troops.   Gen. Polk freely exposed his person,
and displayed great coolness.   Gens. Hardee and Bragg were the life
and soul of the attacking party.   Gen. Gladden had his left arm shot
off, and died shortly afterwards.   Gen. Breckinridge displayed great
military tact and daring, and all the other Generals were active and
fearless.   The enemy's loss was nearly double that of our army.   The
result was the driving of the enemy from their camp and the saving
of Corinth, the capture of artillery, more than twenty-five flags and
standards, and over 3,000 prisoners.

The loud artillery shook the earth, the wood
Seem'd to forego its dreamy solitude.
On, on—brave Johnston gallops to the van,
His flashing eye is turned on every man;
His sword plays with the radiance of the sun,
And, as it glitters, lights you, Southrons, on!
But, see—he falls—mourn, widow'd nation, mourn,
The noblest chieftain of the wars has gone!
But proudly beams his eye in death—he sees
The stars and stripes receding in the breeze.

The day's our own—their camp is our reward,
Our leader now the gallant Beauregard.
With the next sun the struggle was renew'd,
The enemy came up in angry mood,
Bent on regaining all that had been lost,
And driving back our men at every cost.
Stubborn the fight, and, when the sun went down,
Each army held its ground and claim'd the crown.
Thus ended Shiloh's long and bloody fray—
Corinth was free—the foe was kept at bay.

Pulaski fought as long as guns were left *
    To scatter death amid th' invading foe;
A thousand shells her mighty bastions reft,
    And laid her flag and brave defenders low.

---

* Fort Pulaski, after a gallant resistance, surrendered to the Federals
on the 11th April. The surrender was unconditional. Seven large
breaches were made in the South wall of the fort by a battery of eight
Parrott guns at King's Landing. Nearly 1,000 shells were thrown into
the fort before it struck.

And then, at South Mills in the old North State,*
   The gallant Wright sent back the plundering horde;
Many there met a skulking felon's fate
   By bayonet, bullet, cannon shot or sword.
Proud New Orleans, the mart of Southern trade,†
Had long been held in strict and close blockade.
The hostile ships closed in. The sun was high
When Jackson spoke and shook the vaulted sky.
St. Phillip, too, was wreath'd in clouds of smoke
And jets of flame; but soon the stunning shock.
Of thunder claps responded to the roar,
Myriads of shot flew over sea and shore.

---

* A brilliant affair took place at South Mills, N. C., on the 19th April, in which the Confederates were victorious. Col. Wright commanded our forces, and, having heard that the Federals in force of upwards of 5,000 had landed on the night previous, hurried forward with three companies of infantry, an artillery company and one company of cavalry, and attacked them; leaving many of their dead and wounded upon the field, estimated at between 300 and 500. Our loss was 12 killed and 30 wounded.

† The city of New Orleans had long been closely blockaded by a powerful Federal squadron of frigates, gunboats and transports. On the morning of the 24th April this fleet moved up the river towards Fort Jackson, which withstood an immense cannonading. During the night two gunboats passed up along the line of continuous entrenchments and batteries, and suddenly appeared before the city. Commander Farragut demanded an immediate surrender; Gen. Lovell refused, but evacuated the city with his troops, falling back to Camp Moore, leaving the city under the protection of the Foreign Legion. All the cotton and stores which could not be removed, were destroyed. The iron-clad steamer Mississippi was also burnt on the stocks in order to prevent her falling into the hands of the enemy.

Immediately after the fall of New Orleans, Forts Jackson and St. Phillip surrendered after a stubborn resistance. The forts on Lake Ponchartrain were also disbanded and evacuated. This mysterious affair struck the people with astonishment, and many doubts were expressed as to the loyalty of, at least, one of the leading characters; for it was known that the people of the gallant Crescent City rested in security, believing the approaches to their homes insurmountable.

The squadron hurl'd an avalanche of shells,
Each, like a dragon, thro' the welkin yells;
Resistance were in vain—batter'd and worn,
The hush'd guns told the foe their strength was gone.

The fleet pass'd up the stream; the city spires
Were lighted up by skyward flashing fires;
Mountains of cotton, touch'd by flaming brand
To ashes turn'd—the Yankee's contraband.
The city fell—but, firm and loyal still,
Proudly the people scoff'd a tyrant's will.
Butler, "the beast," ruled with despotic power,*
But no one knelt—all were too proud to cower.
Brave chieftain he! with bayonets around,
He warr'd on women—made the world resound
With curses on the wretch whose edict placed
The virtuous maid with those by lust disgraced;
Who hung the man that nobly tore away
The·bloody flag that shamed the light of day.†
Foul offspring of a Puritanic race!
Hath Shame no blush to mantle o'er thy face?
What subtle demon, leaning at thy side,
Whispers to thee—"'T is for thy country's pride?"

---

* One of the first acts of Gen. Butler, on taking the reins of despotic power, was to issue an order which called down the hearty condemnation of all christian nations. In this order he placed the ladies of New Orleans on the footing of common harlots, and gave his myrmidons full license to treat them as such.

† Subsequently he ordered the hanging of Col. Mumford, on the charge of having aided in the heinous crime of tearing down the usurping flag of the United States.

Then fell Fort Macon; to the last her braves *
Plied at their guns, resisting steel-clad boats
And armed hosts, who sought for Southern graves
Dug for them by our balls from iron throats.
At Williamsburg McClellan's monster force †
Attack'd our Johnston—infantry and horse,
With brazen batteries, came thundering down
Toward our works before the classic town.
Twice had we made them fly; the Vermont churls
Had felt the bolt a Southern patriot hurls;
. Dam number two a bloody tale can tell
Of "Mountain boys" who in that struggle fell.
Horse leapt to horse—gun quick replied to gun;
Like bursting clouds, the nimble lightning run

---

* On Friday, 25th April, Fort Macon, on the North Carolina coast, near Newbern, after a bombardment from the enemy's land batteries of ten and a half hours, surrendered. The garrison were allowed the honors of war, the officers retaining their side-arms, and all the men paroled. Seven men were killed and eighteen wounded, two mortally. The enemy's loss was not known.

† On the 4th and 5th May, a bloody engagement took place near Williamsburg, Va., in which the enemy were repulsed with heavy loss in killed and wounded. They also lost twelve pieces of artillery and 500 prisoners. The fight on the 5th lasted from 7 o'clock to 11 o'clock, A. M.
Several severe skirmishes preceded this important battle; they were consequent to the retreat of our army under Johnston from the entrenchments at Yorktown, which it was considered politic to evacuate. The skirmish at Dam No. 2 was sanguine in the extreme, two Vermont regiments having been entirely cut to pieces. The details of the battle give much credit to the troops of Georgia and Louisiana. Gen. McClellan led the invading army, and acknowledged a heavy loss in officers and men, though, as is his custom, he makes a defeat a victory. Our loss was heavy, and Virginia has to mourn the death of many of her bravest sons.
Among our killed were Gen. Early, Col. Mort, Col. Ward, Major Wm. H. Palmer and Captain Jack Humphreys. The 1st Virginia regiment was badly cut up. Out of 200 men in the fight, some 80 or 90 were reported killed and wounded.

In livid shafts along the clashing lines,
While shell tore up the earth like bursting mines.

    For hours the stubborn conflict raged—at length
The charges of our men—their fire—their strength—
Push'd back the foe, they waver'd—broke—they fled,
Leaving the field encumber'd with their dead.
It was a fearful strife—a strife of blood,
Where desperate patriots like a bulwark stood
Defending their homes, their lov'd ones from a foe
That gloated o'er the blood they caus'd to flow.
Oh, triumph dearly won! Many a brave
On that red field hath found a hero's grave;
Many a son, a husband, brother dear,
Sigh'd out his life, no friend his couch to cheer.
Our gallant Early fell—a patriot true,
Mort breath'd his last with victory in view,
Ward, Palmer, Humphreys, sigh'd their latest sigh,
And taught their sorrowing comrades how to die.

    At Sutlington our knotty Jackson dealt
A blow severely by the Yankees felt;*
He drove them back from hill to marsh and wood,
And made them read their errors in their blood.

    Press'd by invading hordes, or some such cause,
(Hist'ry may tell us what the reason was,)

---

* On the 8th May Jackson's advance forces engaged the enemy on Sutlington Hill, near McDowell. After four hours hard fighting, he completely routed and drove them from all points. Our loss was about 300 killed and wounded. Col. Gibbons was killed. The enemy suffered severely.

Our troops abandon'd Norfolk to her fate,*
And Portsmouth too—so fortified of late.
All the stout batteries, where erst they stood
Guarding the quiet city and the flood;
Gosport, with all its works, destroy'd or burn'd,
Its busy shops to desolation turn'd.
Then, as if panic howl'd upon the air,
The great Virginia, wandering in despair,†
No port of safety, plow'd the river waves,
Silent above her former victims' graves.
'T was so decreed; her shot-proof hull was fir'd,
 Her day of glory now had pass'd away;
With one loud blast the gallant ship expir'd,
 She sunk, and left nought but the moaning spray.
Glory too brief—utility scarce tried—
Reigning a day the monarch of the tide.

---

* On the 11th May the cities of Norfolk and Portsmouth, together with the Gosport Navy Yard, were evacuated by the Confederate forces, under Gen. Huger, the latter being for the second time destroyed. Eight or ten Marylanders, under command of Lieut. Spotswood, effectively fired and destroyed the yard. They destroyed every pound of cotton and tobacco they could find in Portsmouth. They also burnt all the steamers and sailing vessels in both ports.

† This splendid specimen of naval architecture, a tower of strength in herself, and which, it was hoped, would contest the entrance of the enemy's gunboats into the mouth of James River, was destroyed immediately after the evacuation of Norfolk. Orders were received by her commander, Capt. Tatnall, to run her up James River, if practicable; and if not to evacuate and blow her up. It was found that her draught was too great to carry her to City Point. She was consequently lightened, her sides being thus exposed, she was unfitted for battle. She was, therefore, beached near Craney Island, and the torch applied. The explosion of her magazine was distinctly heard 25 miles off. Captain Tatnall afterwards demanded a court of enquiry and was acquitted.

Up the James river crept a hostile fleet,*
  For Richmond, ho! they shouted as they sped;
They little dream'd resistance they should meet,
  From rebel guns with pills of moulded lead.
Shelling the shore on either side, they steam'd
Slowly along—their pennons gaily streamed
Over the glassy flood—or hid in smoke
When their huge guns the sleeping echo woke.
Not long that pageant grand. They near'd a bluff
Where watch'd a band made up of knotty stuff,
Who swore to check them on their pleasant route,
And let them know that "rebels" were about.
Boom! and a thousand echoes swell the sound,
Round shot and shell along the waters bound;
The proud Galena reels—her hull's on fire,
She's got her share, and now she may retire.
Crippled they leave their moorings, glad enough
To get without the range of Drury's Bluff.
So, Richmond breathed again—to Yankee wit
She gave full time some other plan to hit.

Again at Giles our champions' arms prevailed,†
A gallant force the Yankee bands assailed,

---

* On the 15th May a brilliant affair came off on James River. The
enemy's gunboats advanced towards Richmond, and were repulsed by
the Confederate gunners at Drury's Bluff—named by the Yankees
Fort Darling. The Monitor and Galena were the leading boats, the
latter was much damaged by our guns, and had to withdraw from the
conflict. Our sharp-shooters also did effective service, picking off
every man who showed himself. The enemy retired, convinced that
they could not reach the capital by that route. We had seven killed,
among them Midshipman Carroll, and eight wounded.

† On May 11th an affair took place at Giles Court House, Va. Gen.
Heth, with 1,500 infantry, 2 guns, one 24 pound howitzer, 4 mountain

Drove them, afright, o'er many a weary mile,
Then left their thieving squads to rest awhile;
While at far Sante Fe our forces proved *
Their pow'r to shield the cause they dearly loved.
  The stout guerilla, on his bounding steed,
Rode thro' the land all fearful in his speed;
His rifle's crack was heard in darksome wood,
His course was traced by streaks of foemen's blood.
The denizens of villages, with fright
Look'd trembling thro' the shadow of the night;
And, when the clattering of a hoof was heard,
They couch'd with fear and utter'd not a word.
"Vengeance" the motto of these daring men,
Their homes were burnt, they now dwelt in the glen.
  Who has not heard of gallant Morgan—he †
Who swore to make his home, Kentucky, free?

---

howitzers and a company of cavalry, started from Shannon Gap to attack the enemy. On reaching the Court House they opened with shot and shell for half an hour, when the enemy fled, and were pursued six miles to Wolf Gap. Our loss was one killed and four wounded. The enemy, it is said, carried off ten wagon loads of killed and wounded.

  * After the battle of Valverde, Gen. Sibley pushed on and occupied northern New Mexico, including Santa Fe. He took Santa Fe on the 15th March, and established his headquarters there. On taking possession he raised the Confederate flag, made of a captured United States flag, on the Federal flagstaff, had a salute fired from the captured Federal battery, and Dixie played on the instruments of a captured United States band.
  Shortly after the occupation of Santa Fe the great battle of Glorietta took place, in which the Confederates were victorious, the enemy suffering, a loss of 700 killed, wounded and missing.

  † Col. John Morgan was the terror of the enemy during the war. He seemed to be omnipresent—and no one knew his whereabouts, until they heard the cry of his fearless horsemen amid the crackling of flames and the roar of fire-arms. He swore to redeem Kentucky, and

Go where the wild deer loves, secure, to roam,
Where erst the red man built his leafy home;
There the ag'd hunter will relate the tales
He'd often heard of steeds that flew on gales,
And phantom horsemen, arm'd with blades of fire;
Who fell on cities with consuming ire;
Laid waste to camps where hated Hessians slept,
And shouted wild as thro' their ranks their swept.
Morgan 's no myth—nor Scott—nor Ashby bold,
Free fighters they, like patriots of old.

Again the wily Jackson trapp'd the foe,*
And at Front Royal laid his standard low,
Captur'd his stores, his ammunition, men,
And made the boaster Banks tramp back again

---

for that purpose gathered a band of dauntless men, with whom he
swept over the country and destroyed everything that might give aid
or comfort to the invaders. Bridges and trains were burned, arms
secured, stores and munitions destroyed, and even cities threatened.

Scott is also another hero of the same class; he with his gallant band
of partizans, performed many daring exploits. He would attack any
force, scarcely stopping to ask its numbers. His exploits on the road
between Tuscumbia and Athens were as brilliant as any on record.

Col. Ashby, of Virginia, was likewise celebrated for his daring feats
as an independent fighter. His untimely death was mourned by the
entire army, and the people felt that they had lost a brave defender and
a stern avenger.

* A great victory was achieved by Gen. Jackson over the Federal
forces under Gen. Fremont at Front Royal, Va. One section of artillery and many prisoners were captured. On the next day Gen. Banks'
main column, whilst retreating from Strasburg to Winchester, was
pierced, the rear part retreating towards Strasburg, and on the following day the other part was routed at Winchester. Brig. Gen. Geo.
H. Stewart with his cavalry and artillery pursued the flying enemy,
capturing many prisoners, and penetrating into Maryland. A large
amount of medical, ordnance and other stores fell into our hands.

Thro' Winchester, with honors closely shorn,
Onward toward his friends at Washington.
The gallant Stewart, with his troopers brave
Pursued the racers to Potomac's wave,
Pass'd into Maryland—gave three loud cheers,
And made the Cab'net tremble with their fears.

 At Lewisburg, Heth with a meagre band *
Put Cox to flight with thousands at command.
Here Edgar fell and gallant Thompson too,
Both dauntless men and to their country true.
And then at Hanover our men attack'd †
A Yankee force by proud McClellan back'd.
The fight was hard; our brigade under Branch,
Contested every inch with foemen staunch;
Five hundred fell with feet toward the foe—
The field was lost—our flag was stricken low.

---

 * The battle of Lewisburg, Va., took place on the 24th May in the streets of the town. Our forces were under the command of General Heth, and numbered about 1,800. The enemy's forces numbered between 5 and 6,000. They were driven from two positions, and then, reinforced, gained a position in Heth's rear, which compelled him to fall back, which was done in good order, across Greenbrier River, the bridge over which they burnt. The Confederates took 75 prisoners, and lost none of their own except the wounded, which were left in the hands of the enemy. Major Edgar, of Monroe, was killed, also Capt. Thompson. Total casualties 200.

 † A severe fight occurred at Hanover Court House, Va., on the 27th May, which resulted in disaster to the Confederates. Our forces were mostly composed of North Carolina troops and one regiment of Georgia, under command of Gen. Branch. After a hard fight of two hours duration, our forces were driven back, a portion of them being badly cut to pieces. The enemy took possession of the railroad between Hanover Junction and Ashland. We had only Latham's field battery in use, two of the guns were abandoned on the field. Our loss was variously estimated from 500 to 1,000.

An old man stood upon the battle field
   When all was still, save dying warriors' groans;
The lips of many a gallant youth were seal'd,
   While there lay gaping flesh and shatter'd bones
In dread array; skulls riven, limbs torn apart,
   And glassy eyes that told of madden'd brain;
While some would on a pool their glances dart,
   And cry for "water!" o'er and o'er again.
A sorrowing youth spoke out to that old sire
   Who mused and ran his fingers thro' his hair,
"Our cause is lost, soon will the flame expire,
   Nought have we now but sorrow and despair."
The vet'ran stood erect, with haughty pride
He scann'd the doubting youth, and thus replied:

Tho' our roofs be on fire, tho' our rivers run blood,
Tho' their flag's on the hill, on the plain, on the flood;
Tho' their bayonets bristle and shots rend the air,
Faint heart! do not utter the cry of despair.

The red moon looks down on the field of the slain,
The gaunt vulture soars o'er the desolate plain;
By the lov'd ones that mantled in glory, lie there,
Arouse from thy stupor and never despair!

We have mountains that lift their gray peaks to the skies,
We have rifles whose crack to the war-yell replies;
We have sinewy arms, we have souls that will dare,
While these are our safeguards, why, doubter, despair?

The great God is just, and he blesses the right,
He makes the weak rise like a giant in might;

When he strikes for his home and the tender ones there,
There's hope in each blow, there is shame in despair!

Then, shoulder to shoulder, push on with a tread
That will shake the loose earth that is heap'd o'er the
        dead;
Bear the torch and the sword to the proud tyrant's lair,
Let the wild battle shout drown the wail of despair.

Despair—while the old man can flourish his staff,
Despair—while the boy at th' invader can laugh;
Despair—while our daughters and wives kneel in prayer,
And our mothers scream out "don't despair—don't
        despair!"

Go, preach to the rock on the lone ocean shore,
And tell it to battle the billows no more;
While there's life, there is hope—for the death-blow
      · prepare,
It is glorious to battle—it is base to despair.

The grandest army of the Northern power,
   Equipp'd in splendor, caparison'd complete,
Led by the "Young Napoleon"—a tower
   Of strength—a polished chief from head to feet,
Came thundering down on Richmond's capitol,
Thro' miry road and over sandy knoll;
Banners of stars and stripes stream'd in the air,
And braying trumpets made the buzzards stare,
While saxe-horn, trombone, ophicleide and drum,
Proclaim'd aloud in swelling tones, "We come!"

This monster army, full of pride and pomp,
At night cross'd o'er a dark and dismal swamp,*
Threw up their works—reserves were at their back,
And then received the daring Hill's attack.

* McClellan's first object on crossing the Chickahominy on his road
to Richmond, 31st May, was to throw up entrenchments of fallen trees,
turf, &c., near Barker's farm. Our forces under Gen. Johnston,
attacked them at that point; Gen. Hill's division led the advance, supported by Gen. Longstreet. With this disposition commenced the battle
of "Seven Pines." Featherstone's brigade led the advance. It was
commanded on the occasion by Col. Anderson, the General being ill.
Garland's brigade commenced the attack on the left, and in a few
moments the engagement became general. After two hours fighting
the Federals were driven from their camps. Our artillery then opened
and made sad havoc among their ranks. The 4th North Carolina, out
of 29 officers, had four killed and nineteen wounded. Capt. Bacon, of
the 27th Georgia, was killed.

The 6th Alabama, 6th Georgia and 23d Georgia suffered severely;
the 6th Alabama being nearly decimated. The 6th Georgia lost 100
out of 500 men they took into the field.

Later in the day Gen. Longstreet's division came into the fight.
Although heavily reinforced, the enemy were charged by the combined
forces of Longstreet and Hill, and driven off the field, our men taking
possession of their camps and fortifications.

Gen. Whiting, while endeavoring to get in the rear of the enemy,
was attacked on the left flank by an overwhelming force, causing him to
change front, and engage in a severe and bloody contest. Hampton's
Legion lost in killed and wounded over one-half its numbers. The
charge of this body of men was gallant and daring beyond all description. Col. Wade Hampton was slightly wounded, and Dr. E. S. Gail-
lard lost an arm. Col. Giles, of the 5th South Carolina, was killed;
also Col. Lightfoot, of the 22d North Carolina.

On the right, during the night, Gens. Hill and Longstreet were reinforced by Huger's division. The enemy were also largely reinforced.
Early in the morning the fight was renewed. Pryor's, Picket's and
Wilcox's brigades stood well up to the front, and were badly cut up,
particularly the 8th and 14th Alabama. Mahone also came upon the
field in good time, fought hard and lost many men; one Alabama regiment alone lost one hundred and ninety-six, killed and wounded.

In this battle the losses on both sides were terrible, shewing the determined resistance of the Confederates to the approach of the "Young
Napoleon" to their Capital.

Not quite content to have so many guests,
To push them back our gen'rals thought it best;
Hot shot, cold steel, used 'freely by our braves,
Gave the proud foe a treat to Southern graves.
Fiercely the fight went on; Longstreet was there,
　And Anderson, and dauntless Johnston too;
Jenkins who "knew his boys" was everywhere,
　Walton the brave—Whiting the staunch and true.
When morning came the struggle was renew'd,
The fiery Pryor the show'r of bullets stood
Till order'd back.　Picket sustain'd the shock
Till Mahone came, as firmly as a rock.
Long hours of slaughter 'mid a noonday's sun,
Both armies stood, and not an inch was won;
The foe was check'd, but sad the tale to tell,
Bacon and Giles, two gallant soldiers, fell;
Hatton and Lightfoot also breathed their last,
To be renowned in stories of the past.

All honor to the gallant men who fought ·
　At Port Republic under Jackson's lead,*

---

*On June 9th Gen. Ewell's command, with a part of Jackson's, attacked Fremont near Cross Keys, five miles from Port Republic. Fremont was repulsed with considerable loss.　On the next day Jackson crossed the north branch of the Shenandoah, above Port Republic, and burnt the bridge.　He then went in pursuit of Shields, who was encamped at Lewistown, two miles below Port Republic, on the east side of the Shenandoah.　He attacked him at sunrise, and, after a terrible battle of four hours, completely routed him, capturing six pieces of artillery (all Shields had) and a number of prisoners.　The rout was as complete as in the case of Banks.　Shields had 9,000 men, and Jackson about the same number.　Fremont was reinforced, and on the same day appeared on the west bank of the Shenandoah, but could not get over to aid Shields, as the bridge had been burnt.

Sustain'd by Ewell, Taylor—chiefs who ought
  To know the foeman's strength—or speed.
A brilliant fight—charge upon charge was made,
Squadrons assailed, contending blade to blade.
Hundreds fell grappling in uncertain strife,
Holding the vict'ry dearer than their life.
For hours the conflict raged, till Shields gave way,
And "Stonewall" once more won a glorious day.
Anon, the hero turn'd his sinewy arm
Toward Fremont—he came down like a storm;
Sent the scar'd traitor, like a beaten cur,
Not back to Mariposa—Winchester!

Stuart, Virginia's pride, with his brigade
Performed a gallant feat, some call it raid,*
Beyond McClellan's lines in front of Lee,
A polish'd son of Southern chivalry.

---

* A military manœuvre unparalleled in the history of war was accomplished about this time. In brilliancy and success it eclipsed the dashing exploits of Morgan, Ashby, Scott or G. H. Stewart.

On the 12th June, Gen. J. E. B. Stuart, with the 1st and 9th regiments of Virginia cavalry, under Col. Lee, one regiment from the Jeff Davis Legion, under Col. Martin, the cavalry from Cobb's Legion, and two pieces of artillery, set out from Ashland on a daring and hazardous adventure. Pursuing a circuitous route, they passed the right of McClellan's lines, and, on the following morning, fell upon a cavalry encampment at Old Church, in Hanover County, about twelve miles from Richmond, and four from the rear of the main forces of the enemy. After a brief contest, the Federal cavalry, consisting of two squadrons, finely mounted and equipped, was routed, and 175 taken prisoners, the remainder fled, leaving their dead and wounded on the field; their encampment was also taken, with a large amount of stores, which were burnt. There being no way of sending the prisoners back to Ashland, their only resort was to carry them on with them. That evening the gallant band, consisting in all of about 2,500 men, reached Hanovertown, on the Pamunkey, where they took four transports by

He led his squadrons bold o'er hill and dale,
With sabre drawn and banner in the gale,
Round to the Yankee's rear for many a mile,
Swept over gully, stony hill and stile,
Capturing scouts and pickets everywhere,
Destroying camps and dealing out despair.
Their ride from Ashland to Pamunkey's flood
Was a long chain of victory and blood.
They burnt three transports with their heavy freight,
Attacked the train, made camp grounds desolate;
Then, with their trophies and a trumpet strain,
They galloped on and reached their home again.
The brave Latane, a noble captain, fell
And, with a war-shout, bade the world farewell.

---

surprise, and destroyed three (the fourth escaping) with their contents, each being heavily laden with army supplies. They continued in a south-eastern direction, and reached the York River Railroad, above the White House, in time to meet the train coming from the rear of the Federal army; and as it approached, they fired into it, killing, it was believed, the engineer and fireman. The train sped on at an incredible speed, and went headlong toward the Pamunkey. After tearing up a portion of the railroad track, they directed their line of march to Charles City County, and began their homeward circuit, the enemy in pursuit. Arriving at the ford over the Chickahominy, they swam the river, patched up an old bridge and passed over the artillery, and were soon out of danger. They arrived in Richmond the day following, bringing with them all their prisoners, about 250 horses and mules, and a quantity of fire-arms and sabres. They only lost one man, the brave Capt. Latane, of the Essex cavalry, who was killed in the engagement at Old Church, where also two men were wounded.

Large quantities of morphine, opium and quinine, were taken from the Federal hospitals. It was estimated that at least one million dollars worth of stores, wagons, tents and other property were destroyed. A portion of the 4th Virginia cavalry were engaged in this brilliant affair.

Now, turn we to James Island, where the foe *
Had lodg'd five regiments of sturdy men,
Who made unlucky haste to strike a blow,
But soon found out they'd struck a tiger's den.
Our dauntless soldiers, led by brave Lamar,
Charleston behind—in front the dogs of war,
Stood the assault—rush'd on with ardor bold,
And gave them back their blows a hundred fold.
'T was a hard fight, the Highlanders pour'd in,
Hot as their fire, with shot and cannon's din,
But vain their efforts, like sear leaves they fall,
And there repose with bonnets, kilts and all.
Vict'ry was ours—a glorious victory;
Again shone bright our star of destiny !
But, mourn we Reed and King, two noble braves,
And Edwards too. Plant laurel on their graves.

McClellan's army met a bloody check
At Williamsburg, again at Seven Pines;

---

* On the 16th June a severe battle took place on James Island, five miles from the city of Charleston, S. C. It is known as the battle of Secessionville. Five regiments of Federals, reinforced by artillery, attacked the batteries at Secessionville. Col. Lamar commanded the Confederates, and with a few hundred troops, repulsed the enemy three times with great slaughter. The Federals fought bravely—but were defeated. Our loss, as near as could be obtained, was about 40 killed and 100 wounded, that of the enemy by far heavier, as our men buried for them 150 left dead on the field, and captured about 70 prisoners. Col. Lamar was wounded. Captains Reed and King and Lieut. Edwards were killed. The Confederate troops engaged were the entire regiment from Charleston, a battalion of the 47th Georgia (Hagood's regiment), Lamar's battery, and a detachment of the Chatham Artillery, of Savannah. The most conspicuous regiment among the enemy, and the one that suffered most, was the New York 79th, the Highlanders—they were badly cut up.

And, tho' he conjur'd "victories" from the wreck
  Of batter'd works and decimated lines,
He learnt a lesson—saw a stubborn foe
  Who'd give up all for sacred Liberty;
Before their wrath his power had fallen low,
  And then he made defeat a "strategy!"
Richmond, the goal of his ambitious schemes,
Was still unconquer'd; there his brilliant dreams
Of proud success concentered—there, thought he,
He'd make the "rebels" bend the pliant knee;
The capital of the Confederate States,
The Rubicon which led to Glory's gates.
But Lee had plann'd, and Longstreet, Jackson, Hill,
Endors'd that cunning plan with right good will;
The cause hung on the issue of the fight,
In God our trust, *he* would protect the right.
  The fray commenced.   Steady and firm the tread
Of Southern troops as up the hill they sped *

---

* The bloody checks which the Northern army, in its memorable
advance up the Peninsula toward Richmond, had received at Williamsburg and Seven Pines, had taught McClellan the desperate character
of the conflict, without which he could never hope to reach, in triumph,
the capital of the Confederate States.   The importance of the series of
Confederate victories will be acknowledged by historians, and as a
summary of the war may here prove interesting, I will engraft one in
these notes.
  A Confederate writer (Clarke) brought his history down to the battle
of Shiloh, and gave the total number of battles up to April 8th, 1862,
at *one hundred and fourteen;* eighty-one of which were Confederate,
and thirty-three Federal victories.   The losses of the Confederates in
all the engagements, sum up as follows: Killed 3,242, wounded 14,530,
captured 21,387.   The Federal loss is thus stated: Killed 12,023,
wounded 20,436, captured 14,279.- Recapitulation—total number of
Confederates killed, wounded and prisoners 39,159; total number of
Federals killed, wounded and prisoners, 46,723.   Number against the
Federals, 7,569:   The largest figures against the Federals are at Shiloh,
viz: 2,500 killed, 9,000 wounded, and 3,700 captured.

Toward entrenchments arm'd on every side
With monster guns that sent a plunging tide
Of canister and shell into their ranks,
While riflemen from pits annoy'd their flanks.
A cloud of smoke obscur'd Mechanicsville—
Onward, still onward, led by fearless Hill,

Fort Donelson is stated thus : Confederates, killed 231, wounded 1,007, captured 3,789. Federals, killed 1,200, wounded 2,000.
Island No. 10 is thus stated : Confederates, killed 3, wounded 3, captured 5,000. Federals, killed 150, wounded 3,000.

The complex character of the movements of both armies in front of Richmond on the three days preceding the great victory of 27th of June, renders a description very difficult to readers who are not familiar with the geography of the country occupied.

On Thursday, June 26th, at 3 o'clock, Major General Jackson took up his line of march from Ashland, and proceeding down the country between the Chickahominy and Pamunkey Rivers, he uncovered the front of Brig. Gen. Branch by driving off the enemy collected on the north bank of the Chickahominy, at a point where it is crossed by the Brook Turnpike. Gen. Branch, who was on the south bank, then crossed the river and wheeled to the right, down its northern bank. Proceeding in that direction, Gen. Branch, in like manner uncovered, at Meadow Bridge, the front of Major Gen. A. P. Hill, who immediately crossed.

The three columns then proceeded en echelon—Gen. Jackson in advance and on the extreme left, Gen. Branch (who was now merged with Gen. A. P. Hill) in the centre, and Gen. A. P. Hill on the right, immediately on the river. Jackson, bearing away from the Chickahominy in this part of the march, so as to gain ground toward the Pamunkey, marched to the left of Mechanicsville, while Gen. Hill, keeping well to the Chickahominy, approached that village and engaged the enemy there.

Driven from the immediate locality of Mechanicsville, the enemy retreated during the night down the river to Powhite Swamp, and night closed the operations of the 26th.

On Friday, 27th, early in the morning the general advance en echelon again began ; Gen. Jackson in advance far to the left, gradually converging to the Chickahominy again ; Gen. A. P. Hill in the centre, and bearing toward New Coal Harbor ; Gen. Longstreet and Gen. D. H. Hill, coming down the Chickahominy to New Bridge. Arrived at Hogan's House, near New Bridge, Gen. Lee awaited the consummation of his magnificent strategy ; courier after courier arrived, informing him of the approach of each division. As soon as Jackson's arrival

Our cohorts dash'd, exposed to raking shot
That plow'd the earth and made the still air hot.
The enemy fell back; their works were ours;
Won by stout hearts 'mid deadly bullet-showers.

---

at Coal Harbor was announced, Gens. Lee and Longstreet, accompanied by their respective staffs, rode to Gaines' Mill and halted at New Coal Harbor, here they joined Gen. A. P. Hill. Soon the welcome sound of Jackson's guns announced his arrival, and the battle began.

The enemy now occupied a singular position, one portion of his army on the south side of the Chickahominy, fronted Richmond, and was confronted by Gen. Magruder; the other portion on the north side, had turned their backs on Richmond, and fronted destruction in the persons of Lee, Longstreet, Jackson and the Hills.

Jackson having begun the contest, it was taken up by the Hills, and raged with great fury and display of the utmost daring and intrepidity by the Confederates from 4 o'clock until 8. The enemy's lines were finally broken and his strong positions all carried, and night covered the retreat of McClellan's broken and routed columns to the south side of the Chickahominy. This retreat continued through Friday night and Saturday morning. Closely watched and pressed by our army, he held his fortified camp on the south side of the Chickahominy during Saturday, 28th, but evacuated it during the night, and resumed his retreat, taking direction toward James River.

The retreat which began from the north side on Friday night, on Sunday changed into a flight, and the *foot races* of the army of the Potomac were run down toward James River, through Charles City county.

On Sunday, June 29th, the battle of Savage Station took place. It was a severe and lively fight, the enemy was easily driven back with loss, many prisoners falling into our hands. The troops engaged on our side were the division of Gen. McLaws, consisting of Gens. Kershaw's and Semmes' brigades, supported by Gen. Griffith's brigade from Magruder's division. Gen. Griffith fell in this fight, which raged furiously until darkness put an end to the contest.

During Sunday, the mortifying fact became known to our Generals that McClellan had in a measure succeeded in eluding us, and was retreating toward James River, having stolen a march of twelve hours on Gen. Huger, who had been placed in a position on his flank, to watch his movements.

On Monday, June 30th, Longstreet, Huger and Magruder pursued the enemy by the Charles City road, with the intention of cutting him off. They overtook him at White Oak Swamp, but they had crossed the stream and burnt the bridge behind them. An artillery fight,

Still forward rushing, in a solid mass,
Our gallant soldiers thro' the village pass,
Assail the second work, by Pender led,·
O'er rifle-pits, abattis, heaps of dead.

however, took place; the casualties on both sides are said to have been severe; indeed it is said to have been the heaviest artillery fight during the war.

At about 4 o'clock on the same day, Gen. A. P. Hill, having command of Longstreet's division and his own, encountered the enemy, who was in position about five miles north of Darbytown, on the New Market road. The fight was desperate, and lasted until half past ten o'clock in the night. President Davis was on the field during the day. During the night the enemy retreated down the Quaker road toward Malvern Hill; here he took a strong position, about two miles and a half from his gunboats on James River.

On Tuesday morning, July 1st, D. H. Hill's division, on the right of Jackson, Whiting, Ewell and Jackson's own division on the left, crossed the White Oak Bridge. Longstreet, A. P. Hill, Magruder and Huger, on the right wing, pushed down the Long Bridge road in pursuit, and took position on the left and front of the enemy, under fire of all his artillery on land and water.

The battle commenced with skirmishers, and soon the entire *corps d'armee* were engaged. The indomitable Jackson assailed the enemy with great energy on the right of their position, and soon drove them from the field. The dusk of evening, deepened into darkness, favored the retreat of the Federals, who succeeded in carrying off their pieces, though with a loss in killed and wounded equal to, if not greater than our own.

On Wednesday, July 2d, the main body of McClellan's grand army reached the much coveted positions in the neighborhood of Berkeley and Westover, on the James River, where they took a rest of more than a month—and then sought a *new base.*

In this series of sanguinary battles, the Federal loss is said to have amounted to over 25,000 killed, wounded and missing. The total of the Confederate loss was 12,989.

Truly does a Northern writer say : " The soil of Virginia is now sacred. It is bathed with the reddest blood of the broad land. Every rood of it, from upper Chickahominy to the base of Malvern Hill, is crimsoned with blood. The dark forests—fitting canopy for such woful sacrifice—echo with the wails of wounded and dying men. There is a bloody corpse in every copse, and mangled soldiers in every thicket of that ensanguined field."

Sons of the old North, Georgia's heroes, too,
Charged side by side and cut their pathway through;
Till Night, in mercy, drew her veil around,
And sent her dews to cool the fever'd ground.

At early dawn the drum, with lengthen'd roll,
Woke the tired soldier—fir'd the drooping soul;
Forward again, more batt'ries to be won,
More blood to flow before the set of sun.
The Hills, brave Longstreet and stern Lee were there;

Pryor and Gregg had hush'd the Yankee's fire;
Our men rush'd on with shouts that rent the air,

Driving th' invading hordes thro' mud and mire,
Till they reach'd Gaines' Mill, where breastworks frown'd,
And monster guns commanded all around.
How cheap was life upon that awful day!
Humanity looked on, then turned away
And wept—for man his savage nature show'd;
In strife slay all you can—that's Honor's code.

On with your firm brigade, brave Pryor, on!
Wilcox, advance! yon batt'ries must be won!
Heed not the storm of grape and canister,
Or shells that pierce the air with fearful blir;
Wave your proud colors—give your war-shout free,
Your country calls—you hold her destiny.

Up the steep hill, with bay'net glist'ning bright,
The brigades rush, then deadly is the fight;
They stagger—halt—brave Wilcox shouts aloud,
"Forward, my boys!" then, 'mid the sulphurous cloud
They disappear, the sod can only tell
How many gallant souls that morning fell.

Yet, onward, tho' a mighty host oppose,
With gallant Featherstone in front, they rose
Above all fear; fainting, tho' fighting still,
.They made their journey up the bloody hill,
When, from the wood, burst forth the gladsome cheer,
"Jackson's come up—he's on their right and rear!"
Terrific now the fight; with furious dash
The columns now in double anger clash;.
Hood with his Texans, Whiting, Pender—sweep
Over the field in blood and carnage deep.
Double the hurricane of fire that shakes
The solid earth—its deaf'ning echo wakes,
Rolls from the foemen's dread artillery,
Sweeping along, like tempest o'er the sea.
Onward we press, and backward fall the foe,
Till their ranks break and their proud flag is low.
Then comes a roar from Jackson's angry guns
    That sends a thrill of terror thro' the mass
Of flying Dutchmen, Puritans and Huns
    Who have permits to leave without a *pass*.
Arms, cannon, baggage, colors—all are lost;
Stores and munitions, that had millions cost,
Are left to us—their gory heaps of dead,
And, with their hosts, their glory, too, has fled!
    Another day set in; more blood must flow
Our forces still pursued the flying foe;
Moody pour'd in his fire near Garnett's farm,
When up came Georgia's vet'rans fresh and warm.
They charge the breastworks, drive the foe beyond,
And, with a cheer, to their faint fire respond—
    11

Yet many a gallant soul fell on that day,
And many a widow weeps her life away.

The holy Sabbath came. Worn, sick with blood,
Our men push'd on thro' paths of mire and mud;
McLaws in front, Kershaw and Semmes' men,
Sustained by Griffith, filed thro' wood and glen.
More grinning bastions barr'd their onward way,
With hot and deadly fire—but what car'd they?
Kemper brought up his death-diffusing dogs,
And ran the Hessians further thro' the bogs.
'T was here that Griffith fell; as brave a soul
As ever courted fire or war-drum's roll;
Mourn'd by the fearless Mississippi band
Who fought at Leesburg under his command.
As the sun set upon the crimson field
Magruder reach'd the flying foeman's rear;
Attacked his ranks, while Kershaw's brigade peal'd
A fire that scatter'd them like frighted deer.
Meanwhile the dashing Stuart made a raid
Toward the White House, captur'd all their stores;
Burnt transports, hosts of prisoners made,
Who mourn'd the day they reach'd Virginia's shores.

With the next morn 't was—up and on again
Toward the White Oaks, o'er a stubbled plain;
There stood the foe with fifty cannon bared,
All loaded, capp'd and for the charge prepar'd.
Our batt'ries open'd, quickly theirs replied,
Death revell'd in the ranks of either side,

Till night closed in. The enemy fell back
And left their dead and wounded on their track.
  Meanwhile the dauntless Hill his corps advanc'd,
Near Darbytown; their bristling bayonets glanc'd
In the bright sun, as firmly on they went
In one huge mass, on victory intent.
The shell and shot whirl'd, whistling, thro' the air,
Devouring fire spread carnage every where;
Mad shrieks and shouts scar'd the wild bird of prey,
And grim Death frolick'd on that awful day.
Still on the victors press'd o'er pools of gore,
Driving with yells the scatter'd foe before.
Night spread around, yet sheets of vengeful flame
Pour'd from the guns, as if from Heav'n they came;
The foe had made a stand, and, reinforc'd,
Essay'd to gain the ground that they had lost.
The shock came on our men with stunning power,
They struggled, 'twas a dark and fearful hour.
Hill dash'd in front of Wilcox's weak brigade,
Bade them cheer loud, the order was obey'd;
The foe was check'd, they thought 'twas Jackson's men,
And so commenc'd their retrograde again.

  Another day set in, and still went on
The carnival of Death; the noonday sun
Saw the two armies drawn up face to face,
One flush'd with hope, the other with disgrace.
The Howitzers and Grimes' batteries
Open'd the ball with cannon melodies,
That made old Earth shake to the very core,
While Heav'n sent back the fierce and doubling roar.

Then came up Pegram, with his veterans bold,
His guns their track of desolation told,
But, one by one they fell, till Davidson
His iron tempest on the foe begun.
Up charg'd a column of our dauntless men,
Like leaves they fell to rise no more again;
Death's whirlwind swept them from the hot plateau;
Cheer upon cheer sent up the haughty foe.
Now the brisk musketry, with fiendish ire,
Sent forth a galling flood of lead and fire;
Appalling thunder leap'd from batteries
That rent the earth and tore the forest trees;
Shells quiver'd in the air from gunboats far,
Death-dealing offerings at the shrine of War;
Squadrons were swept from off the quaking earth,
Carnage and Havoc laugh'd in very mirth.
Our fainting ranks gave way, when, hark, a peal
 Of cannonry upon the foeman's right!
'T is Jackson with his braves! the vaunters reel—
 Break in confusion, then resort to flight!
The veil of night came slowly gath'ring round,
Wounded and dead lie scatter'd o'er the ground;
Zephyrs came dancing o'er the field of gore,
Kissing the dead and whisp'ring—" This is War!"
Fainter and fainter th' hum of flying hosts,
 Louder the cheers of our resistless men;
Where now the "Young Napoleon's" mighty hosts?
 Will they reduce the Capital—and when?
He reach'd his "new base" on James river shore
With half an army—that half sick of war,

Shelter'd by gunboats, spread his canvass out,
And set to work on breastwork and redoubt.
Alas! for that grand host which cost so much,
Alas! for princely staff—French, Irish, Dutch!
Seven long days of battle—nights of woe
Had thinn'd our ranks, but still they watch'd the foe.
Those gallant souls! self-sacrificing braves!
Who at their thresholds found their honor'd graves;
Peace be with them. The poet's harp shall sound
Praise to the dead who fell by Glory crown'd.
Among the many, was the high-ton'd Wheat,
A hero born—a gentleman complete;
Inured to war—he'd been in many a fight,
Ever unflinching, always for the right.
At Gaines' Mills his eagle-eye was seal'd—
His last request—"Boys, bury me on the field!"
Now, rest thee, muse—but half thy task is done,
War's barbed chariot still rolls madly on;
His cry is heard all o'er the groaning land,
And armies melt beneath his blazing wand.

NOTE.—The 2d Canto of the poem of "War" is in course of completion, and will be issued as soon as circumstances will permit.

www.ingramcontent.com/pod-product-compliance
Lightning Source LLC
Chambersburg PA
CBHW021424090426
42742CB00009B/1245